This book is dedicated to John Hipkin, who campaigned resolutely for a blanket pardon to be granted to the 306 soldiers who were shot at dawn by the authority of the Army Act during the Great War; and to the late Ernest Thurtle MP, whose resolve never swayed in his aim to achieve some degree of justice for them; to Andrew Mackinlay; and to the Right Hon. Des Browne, who brought the campaign to fruition.

First published 2014

The History Press
The Mill, Brimscombe Port
Stroud, Gloucestershire, GL5 2QG
www.thehistorypress.co.uk

British Library Cataloguing in Publication Data.
A catalogue record for this book is available from the British Library.

ISBN 978 0 7509 5642 0

Typesetting and origination by The History Press
Printed in Great Britain

Contents

Acknowledgements

I am indebted to the following for helping in the making of this book: Darren Nichols, who has driven me hundreds of miles during the research; the Right Hon. Peter Hain MP, who has kindly written the foreword; Glyn Davies; Martin King; Richard Dyer; Brian Lee; Brian Baker; Lolita McAllister; Derek Vaughan MEP; Dr Paul Davies; Gareth Mathias; Barrie Flint, for drawing the maps; Daniel Smith; the Royal British Legion; the National Memorial Arboretum; Public Record Office; the Imperial War Museum; Leeds University; the Whitehall Library; Ministry of Defence; Declan Flynn and Naomi Reynolds of The History Press; and to my wife, Joy, for all her support.

Foreword

When Robert King asked me in 2006 to support a proposal in the House of Commons to grant a blanket pardon to those soldiers who were shot at dawn in the Great War, I was pleased to do so.

The terrible injustice suffered by 306 British men executed under the Army Act has been like a deep festering sore. Their 'offence' was quite likely to be suffering from shell shock – now called 'post-traumatic stress syndrome'. Through no fault of their own they downed arms and could not serve, so breaching the regulations stipulated by the Army Act. The Shot at Dawn Campaign struggled for years to get recognition and pardons, which were finally granted by the government in which I served in 2006. They were victims of war rather than failures at war.

In the years following the First World War, their cause was raised with great passion in the House: the Labour MP Ernest Thurtle being one of the first to do so, in the early 1920s. He argued that the executed soldiers should be laid to rest in graves alongside those men who fell in action, after responding to a petition submitted by a soldier who felt that they should be honoured in the same way.

Thurtle was successful, and the men who died whilst facing the firing squad were laid to rest with the millions in the impeccably kept cemeteries in Belgium and Northern France.

After Thurtle's time in Parliament, a pardon was raised on a number of occasions until it was finally achieved. But Robert King is not judgmental about the army. The Great War was a bloody, vicious conflict – arguably the worst in history for the sheer scale of casualties: men almost wantonly thrown into action and to their deaths, forced to run 'over the top' to a fusillade of fire and shells amidst the mud and the hideous, pounding chaos. Everyone was under unspeakable pressure as all hell broke loose and they witnessed the carnage, the ugly haunting stench of death everywhere. The officers at the time were adhering to the rules and regulations of the Army Act. Only a shade more than 10 per cent were shot, the rest suffering lesser punishments, though still with the stain of being cowards on their record.

The fact that many of the trial papers were destroyed after the Second World War was used as an excuse for why the subject should not be taken further.

But the Shot at Dawn Campaign persisted nevertheless. The Royal British Legion favoured a blanket pardon with the exception of those soldiers who had been executed for murder. And when it was brought to my attention that a man from my own constituency of Neath had faced the firing squad, my interest was intensified.

Many had no 'prisoner's friend' in support and were not eloquent enough to defend themselves: many were shot as an example to others.

It is important that their stories are told and that their names should be added to the war memorials up and down the country. In very recent times, members of the Campaign have been allowed to march in the parade through London on Armistice Day. I urge anyone who has not visited the National

Memorial Arboretum in Litchfield, Staffordshire, to do so and see the Shot at Dawn Memorial and take note of the very young ages of those men who seem to have cracked under the fearsome pressure and were executed for it.

Robert is to be commended for focusing upon the Welsh soldiers whose stories have not been told and whose memory we salute through this book.

The Rt Hon. Peter Hain
MP for Neath, former Secretary of State for Wales
Ynysygerwn, Neath
January 2014

Preface

My interest in the plight of those unfortunate men who suffered the fate, under the authority of Army Act, of being shot at dawn during the Great War, was ignited when I reviewed the Julian Putkowski/Julian Sykes book, *Shot at Dawn*, in 1989. Absolute ignorance had prevailed in my knowledge in respect of punishments doled out to those who transgressed against the British Army's rules before I was sent the book by its publisher, Leo Cooper. I was familiar with the phrase 'shot at dawn' – it was used often by people in authority, particularly in the early years of the 1960s (by authority I mean those who were training and educating young people in that decade). I worked then in the horse-racing industry in Herefordshire and my employer was Peter Ransom who would, when I failed to muck out stables efficiently or fell off a horse, issue the threat: 'You'll be shot at dawn'. The real meaning passed me by with the process of growing up, but thirty years on it took on a dark shroud: the phrase has haunted the families of the men who were marched out of a building on the Western Front just as dawn was breaking across the French or Belgium landscapes. They were to be faced with a firing squad, usually consisting of men from the unfortunate's own battalion, literally 'blindfolded and alone' – often having been convicted with no mitigation submitted.

I admit I became incensed with what I considered to be an injustice and started to write letters to support the loosely aligned campaign started by John Hipkin, hearing about and understanding the immense amount of work carried out in Parliament and beyond over many, many years by the Labour MPs Ernest Thurtle and Andrew Mackinlay, to secure a blanket pardon for the 306 British and allied soldiers who had been executed.

Then my attention focused on those Welshmen who had been regulars, volunteers or conscripts and then faced a firing squad for committing one of the variety of offences, when, either through in some cases alcoholic inebriation or shell shock (now called post-traumatic stress syndrome). There were fifteen of them: four were convicted of murder, ten for desertion and one for leaving his post. Those men had not been specifically documented in a Welsh context: details of those from England, Scotland, Ireland and other allied countries had been considered, those from Welsh Regiments had not.

It can be very difficult to identify soldiers who served with different regiments – often across the English/Welsh divide. George Povey, for instance, was from Flintshire in Wales but served in the Cheshire Regiment, and a number of Englishmen fought with Welsh regiments. This crossover has been researched as thoroughly as possible but at times it has proved impossible to identify where soldiers originally came from and some may have been missed.

Other documents generally say that of the 306 men, fifteen were Welsh and my research supports those findings.

Executions of Welsh Soldiers and Those who Served in a Welsh Regiment in Date Order

Date of Execution	Service Number	Name	Age	Battalion	Crime
11.2.1915	19459	Private George Povey	23	1/Cheshire	Leaving his post
15.2.1915	12942	Lance Corporal William Price	41	2/Welsh Regiment	Murder
15.2.1915	11967	Private Richard Morgan	32	2/Welsh Regiment	Murder
22.4.1915	10958	Private Major Penn	21	1/RWF	Desertion
22.4.1915	10853	Private Anthony Troughton	22	1/RWF	Desertion

15.11.1915	15437	Private Charles Knight	28	10/RW	Murder
7.2.1916	10874	Private James Carr	21	2/ Welsh Regiment	Desertion
30.4.1916	1/15134	Private Anthony O'Neill	*	1/SWB	Desertion
20.5.1916	12727	Private J. Thomas	44	2/Welsh Regiment	Desertion
5.1.1917	**	Sub-lieutenant Edwin Dyett Nelson	21	Bat. RND	Desertion
15.5.1917	8139	Private George Watkins	31	13/Welsh Regiment	Desertion
25.10.1917	15954	Private William Jones	*	9/RWF	Desertion
22.11.1917	11490	Private Henry Rigby	21	10/SWB	Desertion
10.5.1918	36224	Private James Skone	39	2/Welsh Regiment	Murder
10.8.1918	44174	Private William Scholes	25	2/SWB	Desertion

* In the cases of Private Anthony O'Neill and Private William Jones, their ages cannot be ascertained. It is believed they were both under 18 years.

** As Dyett was seconded into the army from the navy, he was still a member of the Nelson Battalion and so did not carry an army number.

Quotations

The following quotations serve to illustrate the attitude and feeling regarding executions carried out under the authority of the Army Act during the Great War.

Arthur Page describes the conditions of a typical general – or field – court martial. During the war these were held in France in a Nissen hut or a similar structure:

> A table with a blanket over it, and some upturned sugar boxes usually did service for court equipment ... I wish I could portray the scene as the drama unfolds. The dim light of a few spluttering candles throwing into relief the forms of the accused and his escort; the tired and drawn faces of the witnesses under their tin helmets; and the accused himself, apparently taking only a languid interest in the evidence as it accumulates against him.[1]

Percy Winfield describes the different treatment of officers to rankers:

The accused, if an officer, is allowed a seat; if of any other rank, only when the court think proper. It is hard to see how discipline could be injured if this was made a matter of right for all ranks.[2]

Lord Moran on the effects of shell shock:

Courage is will-power, whereof no man has an unlimited stock; and when in war it is used up, he is finished ... His will is perhaps almost destroyed by intensive shelling, or by a bloody battle, or it is gradually used up by monotony, by exposure, by the loss of support of the staunchest spirits on whom he had come to depend, by physical exhaustion, by a wrong attitude to danger, to casualties, to war, to death itself.[3]

Edwin Vaughan on the battlefield:

From the darkness on all sides came the groans and wails of wounded men; faint, long sobbing moans of agony, and despairing shrieks. It was only too obvious that dozens of men with serious wounds must have crawled for safety into new shell holes, and now the water was rising about them and, powerless to move, they were slowly drowning.[1]

Charles Myers on the attitude to shell shock:

[He was] a very young soldier charged with desertion, who had been sent down to Boulogne for a report on his responsibility. He was so deficient in intelligence that he did not in the least realize the seriousness of his position. My only course, I thought, was to have him sent home, labelled 'insane' and the sequel was that he was returned to France with a report saying that no signs of insanity were discoverable in him.[5]

Edwin Dyett's reputed last words when tied to the firing post, naturally fearing the *coupe de grâce:*

For God's sake, shoot straight.[6]

Philip Gibb, a press correspondent, writes from the front in 1917:

... about a young officer, sentenced to death for cowardice (there were quite a number of lads like that). He was blindfolded by a gas mask fixed on the wrong way round, and pinioned, and tied to a post. The firing party lost their nerve and their shots were wild. The boy was only wounded, and screamed in his mask, and the A.P.M. had to shoot him twice with his revolver before he died.[7]

Leon Wolff quoting Philip Gibb on Flanders Fields:

And he continues to say that he encountered more and more deadly depression in the ranks among men who could see no future except more bloodshed. They feared what was to come, they cursed the luck that had brought them to Flanders while other more fortunate fellows were in Palestine, on battle cruisers in the Atlantic, at desks in London, playing at war in Greece, counting boots and cartridge cases at French ports, or a hundred other cushy places; and above all they hated the Salient with a despair reflected even in the place-names: Suicide Corner, Dead Dog Farm, Idiot Crossroads, Stinking Farm, Dead Horse Corner, Shelltrap Barn, Hellfire Crossroads, Jerk House, Vampire Point.

The scene in no man's land during those final days of September was indeed a chilling one.[8]

Chapter One

The Months
Leading Up To The War

The census figures for Wales in 1911 record a population of 2.4 million. The vast majority of the male population would have been employed in heavy industry, including agriculture. When war was declared in 1914, the government launched a patriotic plea asking for volunteers – usually called Kitchener Volunteers – to go to war for king and country. There was no conscription until 1917.

Seemingly bent on conflict, Germany had seriously remilitarised its army during the reign of Kaiser Wilhelm II and started to gather its forces on the border with Belgium. Observing nations concluded that an invasion was imminent, despite Belgium being protected by a guarantee of neutrality. The British Prime Minister, H.H. Asquith, instructed the Foreign Secretary, Edward Grey, to issue an ultimatum: if Germany did not give Belgium an assurance of safety then Britain would intervene on Belgium's side and war would be declared. At that time, the British Empire was still a respected force in the world.

Edward Grey's missive stated that the deadline for this 'assurance of safety' would expire at 11 p.m. on 4 August 1914 which, records tell us, was a hot Bank Holiday weekend.

No assurance was received from Germany, so Britain declared war and the bloody conflict began.

In Wales, 275,000 men signed up during the four years of war, including those conscripted after 1917. Of these, 35,000 were killed and many more were physically or mentally disabled, and left with little or no support.

David Lloyd George was keen to see men from Wales offering themselves as soldiers. To encourage friends to join in groups, Pals Battalions were established, which kept men from the same area together. However, this meant that they also died together – thus the large number of names on war memorials that populate almost every village. This idea was not propagated during the Second World War, when efforts were made for fighting men from same area to be kept apart, particularly if they were related.

With patriotic fervour sweeping the whole of Britain in the days and weeks following the declaration of war, men in their thousands volunteered. The idea that it would all be over by Christmas was bandied about and it was seen as an adventure, an attractive change from the norm. The actual realities of what they were signing up to came later, by which point there was no backing out of the commitment.

In Wales the majority of the male working population was employed in coal mines, quarries and agriculture. The wages were poor and living conditions were sparse, and so many young men willingly took the king's shilling. Women took over many of the duties previously performed by the menfolk and children were encouraged to help the war effort by collecting conkers.

There was considerable excitement for those queued up at the recruitment offices. It was difficult to resist the accusing finger pointing out from the War Office posters, which proclaimed 'Your Country Needs You', or to ignore the undercurrent of encouraging young women to present those men still not in khaki with a white feather – the symbol of a coward.

The pressure was extreme, as was described by Private Rhys Davies of Carmarthen. I spoke with Mr Davies in 1973:

My brother, Gareth, had signed up immediately when they asked for volunteers. He was four years older than me and couldn't wait to go. We were both farm labourers working on different farms just outside the town. I remember Gareth saying when he told my mother he was going that he'd been to Swansea once, now he had the chance to go overseas. I was a bit jealous; although I looked older than my seventeen years I was resigned to wait. That was until I was walking in the town one night and this girl put a white feather into the top pocket of my coat.

'A Welsh coward,' she said. She was with five other girls who all giggled and made fun of me. I went bright red with embarrassment and stuttered I'm only seventeen.

'That's what they all say,' she added and tried to give me another feather. She must have had a load of them in her handbag.

I was shaking with temper, turned and ran home. That white feather business was evil.

Anyway, the following day was the market and I knew I'd be able to have an hour off but I told no one what I was going to do.

When I got to the recruiting office there was a queue, about five or six of us. I knew a couple who had been friends of my brother but no one said anything. I think everyone was a little nervous or so excited they couldn't talk.

The sergeant called my name and took details. I told him I was born in 1897; it was a lie, I was born in 1898. Then a doctor examined me and that was it. I was Private Rhys Davies.

I hurried back to the market and helped my employer to take some sheep home then I told him that I had joined the army and wouldn't be working at the farm again. He went quiet. Then, completely out of character he said: 'Good boy,' and he gave me the money I was owed plus a ten shilling note. I was shocked at that and gave the ten bob to my mam.

It was those girls and the white feather that done it.[9]

Private Bryn Thomas from Tonypandy explained to me in the late 1960s that he was 28 and home on hospital leave in November 1915, when he was subjected to the humiliation of having a white feather handed to him 'by a woman old enough to be my mother':

I joined the army in 1912 to do something different really. I'd worked in the pits for a couple of years and got danted with it so I signed on.

When the war broke out then I found myself in Ypres, first off digging trenches. And then as the weather turned and things started getting nasty with the Germans those trenches got wetter and wetter, muddier and muddier until even our bolt holes got uncomfortable.

One night I was huddled deep in my hole, trying to snuggle into my clothes to keep warm, although they were lice ridden you get used to it, when I got a bloody rat bite on my leg. It pinched so much that I put my hand down straight away and caught the bloody thing and squeezed the life out of it. Working in the mines an old collier had once told me that a female rat's bite is worse that a male's so I turned it up and checked what it was. It was a male. But the wound swelled up and I was sent to the dressing station. From there they sent me home for a couple of weeks to give it time to heal. It was nice to get home.

Some soldiers liked to keep the uniform on even when on leave. I didn't, soon as I got in to the house it was a hot bath in front of the fire and my own clothes.

I went down to Pontypridd to see my uncle a few days later and walking to a pub this woman stopped me and said I should be ashamed that I wasn't at the front. I was shocked at this total stranger and then she gave me a feather. Uncle was in a temper. He ripped it from me and argued with her. A few people had stopped at the raised voices. 'The man's a regular,' he shouted and threw it on the ground. 'Come on, Private,' he said, 'a pint, enough of this nonsense.' The woman, red faced, hurried away.[10]

Private Colin Phillips from Ruthin related his experience with a stoic nature when he agreed to talk to me in 1974:

I'd survived the Battle of Mametz Wood so anything anyone ever said to me after that didn't matter much. Yes, a man, a minster of religion in fact, challenged me when I was on a leave. I was in my civilian clothes and he came on to me asking me if I felt ashamed. I knew what he meant and I treated him with distain. I didn't say anything. I just looked at him with contempt. His white dog collar glistening, clean. I thought of the filth and carnage I'd been through and walked away. I never cared much for religion or anything after that. I even struggled with it when attending funerals in later years. I shouldn't consider them all like that man who condemned me without knowledge. But there you are, as my mother always said, there's good and bad wherever you look, everywhere.[11]

The above examples illustrate the emotional pressure placed on young men. The white feather syndrome was encouraged by government ministers to leave the public in no doubt that young men not in uniform were to be branded cowards.

In Wales, as in other parts of Great Britain, the conditions for most working-class men were very poor. In South Wales the mining industry was the major employer – a dangerous occupation which little changed after the Great War. The years between 1894 and 1914 recorded 1,275 fatalities in the South Wales coalfield. A conservative figure, it does not feature smaller incidents where only one or two miners lost their lives. The outbreak of war came a little under a year after the disaster at the Universal Colliery in Senghenydd on 14 October 1913 in which over 400 miners died, so it is unsurprising that joining the army was attractive; although miners worked in an exempt industry they volunteered in their thousands. They were sought by the Ministry of War because of their ability to dig tunnels in a safe and methodical manner, and the tunneling under no-man's-land towards the German lines was principally carried out by those miners with coal-mining experience. Many would have been from South Wales.

Quarry workers in North Wales endured equally appalling and dangerous conditions and farmhands toiled in humbling and exhausting circumstances. Altogether, 275,000 men either volunteered or were conscripted from Wales in the First World War. Of these, 35,000 lost their lives on the Western Front, with fifteen men being shot at dawn following court martial. Four were members of the Royal Welsh Fusiliers; three belonged to the South Wales Borderers; six in the Welsh Regiment; one in the Cheshire Regiment; and one, an officer, in the Royal Naval Division. Two Welsh regiments had no members executed: the Monmouthshire and the Welsh Guards.

The figures for British soldiers from the Home Nations who faced a firing squad (allowing for those who served in another country's regiment) were: 24 Irishmen, 43 Scotsmen and 209 Englishmen.

Under the authority of the Army Act, offences carried more severe punishments when a soldier was on active service. The generals felt the only way to maintain essential discipline was by imposing severe penalties.

Chapter Two

The King's
Shilling

Taking the king's shilling committed a soldier to live under the authority of the Army Act, which enabled the military to enforce punishments for offences in the field that did not apply in civilian life. Whether the reality of the strictures of the Army Act was thoroughly digested by the willing volunteer is not known as many of the oral statements we have at our disposal are reflective – their attitudes may have changed since they presented themselves at a recruitment office. It is well known that recruitment officers were generally vague in their definition of the procedures of recruitment.

Many young men lied about their age, with some as young as 14 signing up. There were many 'men' signing up who were mere boys, but if the heart was willing, etc., then a blind eye was turned – the numbers game was paramount. The Army Act protected the officers in this respect: the age of every recruit was taken to be accurate, and so what the young men said was just taken to be true.

The clamour for excitement, the show of bravado and the belief that it would be over by Christmas shows on the faces of the young men captured on film footage as they stand on board ships heading for France, the faces smiling and anticipating the forthcoming adventure. Many leaned against the rails of the ships' decks, waving to whomsoever and not realising what lay in store.

Reality proved their expectations far from the truth, and some grew disobedient or resorted to desperate measures to escape. Death by firing squad accounted for 349 soldiers during the Great War, found guilty of committing the offences of:

Desertion	Striking an officer
Cowardice	Sleeping on duty
Leaving their post	Mutiny
Casting away arms	Murder
Disobedience	Rape

Through the duration of the war there were 750,000 Allied soldiers killed (an average of 400 a day) and more than 1,500,000 wounded. For the sake of example, there were more than 3,000 men condemned to death for contravening the regulations of the Army Act, but only slightly more than 10 per cent were carried out.

It seems a tiny percentage of the war's losses, but the soldier's realisation that in trying to escape going over the top he was going to be put to death in the morning by members of his own side would have been devastating. Witnesses to those dark moments in British history often paint a picture of an immense stoical power.

A medical officer offered one man a heavy drink of spirits in an effort to numb his mind, minutes before he was led out to face his end; the response was that he'd never taken hard drink in his life and he saw little point in starting now. A minority refused to be blindfolded and chose to face the wrath of the firing party – one chaplain recorded that he had never seen a braver soldier facing his death. Alternatively, some soldiers were injected with morphine to dull their senses. Not all were so stoic, often in the case of the very young men, the youngest being 16 years old: Private Highgate of the Irish was 16 years and 8 months old. Soldiers such as he would have volunteered by lying about their age, again having been caught up in the excitement of adventure, and the prospect of facing a firing party would have been horrific. One pathetically cried out as he was being tied to the firing post, 'What will my mam say?'

Knowing that executions were carried out in civilian life as an example to others – such as hanging men found guilty of committing capital offences – but were not an effective deterrent, it is tempting to ask why firing squad was used at all. But in the context of the time, the army was still operating under the rules of the late nineteenth century when life was considered cheap.

Considering the stresses that new recruits and indeed regular soldiers were experiencing with trench warfare, many of the 3,000 men found guilty of offences carrying the death penalty would have been suffering from psychological conditions not recognised by medical practitioners of the time. Although shell shock was documented, it was not considered a mitigating factor in any defence that was offered.

Contrary to the legal requirements in civilian life – of innocent until proven guilty – the army followed the mantra of guilty unless proven innocent. The trial process was haphazard, not so much for prosecuting officers but very much for defendants. Many men facing the life or death decisions of the prosecutors were often unrepresented, or at best represented by men who were not equipped with knowledge of presenting mitigation. This knowledge, often called a 'soldier's friend', was not so much denied as not requested by the soldiers who were, no doubt, in ignorance of its existence.

Until 1915 a defendant would plead guilty, which sealed his fate. This was only to change with the case of Private Joseph Byers, a Kitchener volunteer aged 17 who had joined the

1/R Scots Fusiliers. He made a 'guilty' plea of Attempting to Desert at his Court Marshal, had no defence and claimed he did not know what he was doing. He was executed for desertion on 6 February 1915 and was buried at Locre Chyd. Following this case, all soldiers facing a court martial had a 'not guilty' plea automatically imposed.

Some defendants offered up in mitigation that he had been shell-shocked, 'a shell went off next to me and my mind went strange' or 'I couldn't see or think after a shell went off behind me'. If this was in the hope that a medical examination would find that he was not mentally in charge of his faculties and so a doctor would support him, his hopes would have been dashed when he was rudely made aware that doctors would be of no support. One doctor recorded that he found such people repugnant and cowardly and 'I hate his sort'. The soldiers soon found themselves nearly blindfolded and alone.

If the prosecutors found the defendant guilty but made recommendations that the death penalty should not be carried out, and this was supported by the commander in chief – most notably Sir Douglas Haig – the soldier was informed of his punishment. He knew his fate relatively quickly. But if the death penalty was approved, the man would sit in his cell or holding place quite ignorant as to what was to become of him. When the orders came through (and the length of time from the trial's end and conformation that the man was to be shot varies greatly from case to case) the soldier was informed on the evening before his execution on the parade ground. He would then have been ushered away to his cell.

The condemned would be attended during that night by the chaplain, who did in some cases help with letter writing and offering what comfort he could.

The next task for the officer in charge was to assign men to the firing squad or party. These were usually made up of six men, although some accounts record as many as twelve this would certainly have been unusual. It must have been horrendous to be instructed to carry out this duty; in some cases the members of the firing party would have known the condemned. To be involved in a firing party would often leave a mark on a man who had knowingly shot someone who had been fighting on the Allied side. Members of the battalion would often be forced to observe the event, to remind them of the consequences of their actions.

If members of the firing party did not kill the condemned man outright and the victim was left wounded and not dead, then the officer in charge would move forward. After the medical officer had pronounced that the man was still alive, the officer would produce a pistol and shoot the victim in the head. It is easy to see why Sub Lt Edwin Dyett was so anxious that his firing squad shot straight.

The body was then placed in a sheet and taken away and buried, sometimes in a makeshift grave, which was marked for reburial in a cemetery later. On some occasions the original grave's location was lost and then the name was just commemorated on one of the remembrance walls.

In many cases the fact that a soldier had been executed wasn't conveyed to the family: the communication would only read 'died of wounds'. On receiving such a missive, some families placed a picture of the deceased in the windows of their homes, but if the relatives discovered the truth the picture was hurriedly removed. One widow, who had received the news from the War Office that her husband had 'died of wounds', enquired about the pension she thought she would receive but was bluntly informed that the government did not pay pensions to cowards. The medals and death plaque were also withheld.

Having a relative shot at dawn was devastating and many families disappeared from their home villages or towns because of a feeling of shame. Those executed soldiers often disappeared from history. Yes, the record was retained by the

War Office (unfortunately many of these records were lost during the Blitz of the Second World War) but locally, at the end of the war when memorials started to appear throughout the country to commemorate the fallen, their names were omitted. Indeed, Julian Putkowski and Julian Sykes in their book *Shot at Dawn* actually apologise to those families who might find out through reading the book that their relatives had been executed, in case the information was unknown or had been kept secret by the family.

No matter the offence that had been committed and led to the execution, be it cowardice, desertion, murder or rape, the body of the soldier was treated in the same way in the communal cemeteries as those who had fallen in action. Only one grave in all of the Western Front cemeteries carries the words 'Shot at Dawn' – that of Private Albert Ingram of the Manchester Regiment. On a Commonwealth War Graves Commission headstone, families are allowed to place a brief inscription to accompany the name, rank, regiment and date of death. When the father of 10495 Private A. Ingram of the Manchester Regiment, who was executed on 1 December 1916, eventually knew the truth about his son's death, he ordered that the words: 'Shot at Dawn – One of the First to Enlist. A Worthy Son of his Father', be inscribed.

Following the blanket pardon in 2006 of the 306 soldiers who were executed for all offences, with the exception of murder, mutiny and rape, the names have started to appear on the memorials but usually following local campaigns.

It has become recognised that post-traumatic stress is a reason for those soldiers transgressing the army's regulations. A lack of adequate representation for any sort of mitigation to the prosecuting officers added to so many being found guilty and shot.

In respect of the burial and commemoration of those executed, the Imperial War Graves Commission – later renamed the Commonwealth War Graves Commission – communicated with the War Office in 1922, requesting the names of those soldiers who had been shot.

> The Commission would be greatly obliged if they could be furnished with a list of soldiers who had been executed by Field General Court Martial during the late War, with the dates of execution and if possible the places.
>
> It should be explained that the names of these soldiers are not given in the publication 'Soldiers Died in the Great War'. The Commission has however decided on consideration to erect headstones of the usual pattern, over their graves without any reference to the manner of their death, or, if their graves are not known, to commemorate them in the same way as other officers and men whose graves are unrecorded, and it is therefore necessary to apply to you in this manner in order to be sure that the Commission's records are complete.[12]

The War Office expressed no objection to the request, which suggests that it had no intention and was not attempting, as it has often been accused, of covering up the fact that men had been executed in the theatre of war on the Western Front. The reason that the men's names were omitted from the publication 'Soldiers Died in the Great War' was to afford some measure of protection to both the executed and their families.

The War Office's view was that those men who had been shot at dawn had paid their debt and should now lie side by side with their fallen comrades.

A Public Record Office missive expands on the subject:

> *Burial procedure to be adopted after cases of judicial execution carried out under military arrangements*
> There should be nothing to prevent the burial of a victim of judicial execution in a military cemetery.

Soldiers who are judicially executed at a time when death of a soldier qualifies them for war graves treatment are treated like other soldiers. But since executions for say, desertions, are not made public, the question of public opinion being outraged at the burial side by side of a soldier executed for desertion and of another who died gallantly in action, does not arise.[13]

It appears that some families were made aware that their menfolk had been executed, but there seems to have been a degree of sincerity in the reasoning that to publish the fact would only have served to add to the grief of the relatives.

Chapter Three

Executed For
Leaving His Post

10459 Corporal George Povey became the first Welshman to
be executed and the first soldier to face the firing squad for the
offence of 'leaving his post'.

George Povey was born in Hawarden, Flintshire in 1892.
On his enlistment in 1914, he was a single man living in
Connah's Quay. He joined the 1/Cheshire Regiment as a
regular soldier and had been sent to France soon after joining
the army. Testament to his ability and good record, he attained
the rank of corporal in a short period of time. This undoubtedly was a source of pride to him but would ultimately lead to
him 'carrying the can' and facing the firing squad.

Since the beginning of the war there had been several
men sentenced to death for quitting the post, but they had
all had their sentences commuted to a period of imprisonment. The most extreme of these was Private Cunningham
of the Essex Regiment, who had been condemned to death
for leaving his post on two occasions. His sentence was commuted to ten years' penal servitude. Corporal George Povey of
Connah's Quay was not to be so lucky.

Corporal Povey was in charge of four men as they defended the line near Wulverghem, when it seems that the Germans penetrated the defences and a shout went up that they were in the trench. Absolute panic reigned. It was during the early hours of the 28 January and, on hearing the confusion, some men who had been asleep made their way towards the rear, but were stopped at a support point when they were instructed to return to their posts.

Corporal Povey and his men were among them. On being ordered to return to his post, he did. Apparently the panic had started when a lone German soldier had pulled a rifle through a hole and everything erupted. Povey said he heard the words on the very cold January morning, 'Clear out, lads, they're on us.' He had been asleep – legitimately, it seems, because he used the fact in his defence – and woke suddenly, saw men running and joined them, together with his four privates.

At his trial he said he had been asleep and that when ordered back to his post he had done so and that he had with him all the time his rifle and arms. The witnesses speaking on Povey's behalf were probably the four privates under his supervision. They proved inadequate, uttering no more than a few words between them.

The outcome of the court martial was that the four privates were found guilty of quitting their post and were sentenced to ten years' penal servitude, with strong recommendations for mercy. The recommendation was acted upon and the four men were given periods of imprisonment.

However, Povey – being the non-commissioned officer (NCO) – was sentenced to death. It is quite likely that he was the first officer in charge to have faced this offence and the army's Manual of Military Law states that an NCO should be punished more severely than a private for committing the same offence. As an NCO he should have attempted to ease the panic that ensued around him and not joined in with it.

Povey's situation was hopeless. He was not going to see North Wales again. The case officers implemented the Military Law Manual's guidance notes and the army commander wrote that 'this is a serious case and I agree with the Corps Commander that the death sentence should be carried out'.

His hard work and promotion had in fact acted against him as it meant the punishment was not merely a period spent in jail.

George Povey was executed at St Jan's Cappel on 11 February 1915. His immediate grave was lost during the confusion of the war and his name is commemorated on the Menin Gate. He was 23 years of age.

Chapter Four

Executed
for Desertion

Desertion was considered one of the most serious offences that could be committed under the confines of the Army Act. It was deemed to be calculated and deliberate as opposed to cowardice, which could be seen as a lapse in a man's resolve. Thus there were far more executions for desertion than any other crime.

During the entire period of the war there were nearly 127,000 court martials held for the offences of desertion and absence. The most common means by which a soldier could desert was to not return to his unit following home leave. During the early part of the war the names of deserters were published in the *Police Bulletin* and often these names would be picked up by the popular press. Thus a man on the run would have had little chance of evading capture. Nevertheless some did and they would go to extreme measures of hiding their identity. They could change locations, their name, etc. Naturally, the more common surnames were difficult to locate and many men were successful in getting themselves lost in the general population of Great Britain.

Section 12 of the Army Act is quite clear on its attitude to desertion. A missive issued by the War Office states:

... absence without leave with the intention either of never returning to the service at all or avoiding some particular onerous or dangerous duty ... differs from cowardice in that it involves a definite and specific intention. It need not occur in the presence of any danger and is more likely to be the result of a calculating regard by a man for his own safety than cowardice which is inspired by fear in the presence of actual danger.[14]

There runs a fine line between the offences of absence without leave, desertion or even quitting the post. This was often the problem for prosecuting officers at court martial in the field. In the case of Corporal Povey it can be argued that he responded to a call to 'move back', that is, he did not knowingly quit his post. And in Edwin Dyett's case (*see* Chapter Five) he had refused to take an order from a lower-ranked officer and had gone back to his base for further instruction. Nevertheless they had been deemed to have absconded, no matter what criminal label was attached to them. They paid with their lives.

The first executions of Welshmen, or men who were not of Welsh descent but serving in a Welsh regiment, took place on 22 April 1915.

10958 Private Major Penn and 10853 Private Albert Troughton, both regular soldiers and single men serving in the 1/Royal Welsh Fusiliers, became the fifth double execution of the war. Both were Englishmen. Major Penn (Major was his Christian name) was born in 1894 near Stourbridge in Worcestershire and had signed up at the age of 17, joining the Worcestershire Regiment. Clearly at some stage between joining the army and his execution, he had been rerouted or transferred to the Royal Welsh Fusiliers. He was 21 when he was shot.

Albert Troughton was born in Foleshill, Warwickshire in 1893 and was 22 years old when executed.

Both had been involved in the fighting around Ypres when the battalion of 300 or so soldiers came under an intense attack from the Germans who, it seemed, had almost penetrated the Allied line. The commanding officer, according to Troughton, told him that his brother had been killed along with hundreds of others in the attack. Troughton said that his commanding officers shouted, 'Everyone for himself,' so Troughton and, one assumes, Penn, wandered off.

With, it appears, no one to substantiate Troughton's claims as members of the battalion were either dead or in German hands, he, along with Penn, was found guilty of deserting his post.

Penn had joined the army when he was 17 years old and he and Troughton had good records. But this did not mitigate in their favour when Douglas Haig confirmed the sentence of death as a deterrent to others.

They are buried side by side in Estaires Communal Cemetery, Belgium.

Joe O'Loughin publishes on his website a letter Troughton had written the night before his death. Poignantly and bravely, he lets his parents know that tomorrow he is to be shot. He says that he will die like a soldier and pray for them. He says that he shouldn't have wandered off but his mind was everywhere.

Little wonder, having received the information that his brother was dead amid all the carnage of the attack. He seems to have accepted his fate and ends his last letter home with the words, 'Goodbye, Goodbye.'

Private James Grist Carr

Private Carr was a regular serving in the 2/Welsh 1 Division. He was born in Gloucestershire and had been an unmarried errand boy when he joined his regiment as a regular soldier at the outbreak of the war. The circumstances surrounding his alleged desertion are vague to say the least – another set of documents destroyed during the bombing of London during the Second World War.

Private Carr's military record was unblemished. And his execution seems to have been a somewhat hurried affair because only two weeks after his trial he was led out and shot. He did not help his own case because, whilst under arrest, he escaped only to be recaptured almost immediately.

He was executed in the French village of Auchel on the morning of 7 February 1916 and lies buried in Auchel Communal Cemetery. He was 21 years of age.

Private Anthony Victor O'Neill

1/15134 Private Anthony Victor O'Neill (some documents spell his surname as Neil) was a Kitchener volunteer serving with the 1/South Wales Borderers. I have failed to find a record for this soldier on the 1911 census. Equally, the reasons that led to his desertion are sketchy or non-existent.

Private O'Neill joined the army in November 1914 and seems to have had a clean record sheet. His court martial found him guilty but recommended mercy on account of his good record. This recommendation was not acted upon and he was shot in the Mazingarbe abattoir on 30 April 1916. He is buried in the Mazingarbe Communal Cemetery Extension. His age is unknown. When visiting the Shot at Dawn site at the National Memorial Arboretum in Litchfield, Staffordshire, I enquired about the fact that some of the victims commemorated on the posts had their ages omitted. An officer on the site said that when the ages were omitted it was believed that they were grossly underage.

So Private Anthony O'Neill could have been in his mid to late teens when executed. Considering his youth, he was probably an unmarried man. But, to complicate the lack of factual evidence regarding his age, his being a reservist indicates that he was much older.

Private John Thomas

2727 Private John Thomas was a reservist with the 2/Battalion Welsh Regiment 1 Division.

Private Thomas was 44 years old, a native of the Pembrokeshire village of Lamphey and married with three children. As a reservist he was called into action at the outbreak of war, landing in France in February 1915. He was part of the offensives at Neuve Chapelle and the Second Ypres.

He clearly felt aggrieved, considering his age, that he was posted to fighting on the front line, feeling that his senior age should have given him work behind the lines. Unlike many of the volunteers and young recruits, he would have been fully aware of the consequences of deserting when he left the ranks in the spring of 1916. He was soon captured. In his defence he argued that, being much older than the majority of soldiers in the ranks, he found it difficult to keep up with them and had expected to be given a job behind the front line.

The argument was not received sympathetically, nor was his marital status nor that he was the father of three children. He was condemned to death.

He was executed on 22 May 1916 in the abattoir in Mazingarbe. He is buried in the Mazingarbe Communal Cemetery Extension.

Private Thomas was one of only five soldiers executed over the age of 40 years, and at the age of 44 he was the second oldest man to face the firing squad. The oldest solider was Private Hendricks of the 2/Leinster Regiment, who was shot on 28 August 1918 for desertion at the age of 46 years.

Those who would have faced a court martial above the age of 40 years would quite likely have used their age as mitigation, which could have been considered favourably.

However, not in Private John Thomas' case.

Private George Watkins

8139 Private George Watkins was a reservist with 13/Welsh Regiment who had initially joined the army in 1904, then was recalled to join the service at the outbreak of the war. It has been difficult to identify his hometown or village.

From what information we have, it is established that he had a very good record up until his desertion in 1916. Within days of rejoining he found himself in France. He was involved in the retreat from Mons and in the fighting during the winter months. In 1915 he was twice wounded and then returned to the action following a period of convalescence. He deserted his battalion, which was resting behind the lines, in the December of 1916 and was on the run for more than four months. He was arrested sometime in March 1917.

At his court martial he reminded the panel about his very good record as a serving soldier, and also that he had been beset with family trouble and did not know what he was doing.

This cut little drift with the officers and he was condemned to death.

He was shot on the 15 May 1917. He was 31 years of age and lies buried in Ferme-Olivier Cemetery.

Private William Jones

15954 Private William Jones, 9th Battalion Royal Welsh Fusiliers, was a Kitchener volunteer who hailed from Glynneath, a village in the Vale of Neath. Because of difficulty in finding his name on the 1911 census, we do not know how old he was. The fact that he was a Kitchener volunteer and probably caught up in the euphoria to join up at the start of the war indicates he was very young. The information provided at the National Memorial Arboretum in Litchfield carries no reference to his age, thus leading us to believe that he was very much underage when he was executed. There are references telling us that he was from Neath and this is supported by local information, mostly passed down orally from generation to generation, and I have been given a fading sepia photograph of him by a distant relative living in another part of Wales. Also the Glynneath Branch of the Royal British Legion is supportive of the fact that he was from their village. Mr Brian Baker of that branch has been most helpful in various ways regarding the biography of this soldier, who was quite likely only fluent in Welsh. His English was probably sparse, which would not have been unusual coming from this part of Wales.

Jones was a stretcher bearer in France who went missing on 15 June 1917 after taking a wounded soldier to the dressing station. The job of a stretcher bearer entailed going out into no-man's-land collecting wounded and dead soldiers and their body parts, and returning them to the dressing station. It was a horrendous duty for such a young man and it could have unhinged him, causing him to desert.

Whatever the truth of it, he went missing and became one of only eight soldiers who deserted and were detected having managed to cross the English Channel to return to Britain. What we do know is that he turned up in Glynneath and, by dint of his name alone, he could have remained undetected. At that time there were upwards of forty gunners named W. Jones serving with the Royal Welsh Fusiliers alone (I have found one other William Jones, a serving soldier, whose home address was Neath at the same time). Indeed, another soldier called William

Jones serving with the 43rd Battery, Royal Field Artillery had been shot at dawn for desertion on 20 April 1915. (He was not a Welshman and I make reference to this case only to illustrate the proliferation of the name).

Private William Jones was away from his battalion for about three months. During the early days of September 1917, he handed himself in to Neath Police Station and the officers there promptly sent him to the assistant provost marshal in Bristol. If he had not made the decision to surrender it is probable that he would have been undetected for the duration of the war. The powers that be, including the army, would not have had the resources to diligently track down a soldier on the run. It would have been to his advantage to continue using his given and family name.

But he did give himself up and told the officer in Bristol that he had been wounded in France and evacuated to England. His trial found no evidence of this. Judge Anthony Brabington in his book *For The Sake of Example* states that Jones' company commander had said at the trial that he had been with the battalion ever since they landed in France and hitherto had proved himself a good soldier.

We will never know the reasons that provoked him to submit to the authorities. Whether he thought that handing himself in would be considered in his favour in the trial, or that he had been a Kitchener volunteer would also help his case, was sadly mistaken. Of course, volunteers, reservists and conscripts were all treated in the same way under the army's disciplinary procedures.

Private Jones was executed on 25 October 1917 on Kemmel Hill and his body lies in the Lochre Hospice Cemetery. He was probably under the age of 18.

The fact that William Jones was from Neath, my home town, accelerated my interest in the subject. Following the blanket pardon that had been secured in the House of Commons in

2006, initiated by the Rt Hon. Des Browne, the defence secretary, I strove immediately with others to have his name placed on the war memorial at Glynneath. It had been omitted along with all the other men from all parts of the United Kingdom who had been executed in the Great War: their names wiped from memory.

Brian Baker of the Glynneath British Legion was naturally very keen to have Jones' name recorded on the memorial. On 9 November 2006, he received a communication from The Royal British Legion called: 'Legion Statement re Pardon for WWI Soldiers Shot at Dawn', which read:

> The Royal British Legion welcomes the Defence Secretary's announcement that parliamentary approval for the pardoning of the 300 plus soldiers executed for military offences during the First World War has been given.
>
> We have always acknowledged that it is very difficult to get to the roots of this sensitive and difficult matter and we accepted Dr John Reid's statement, made in 1998, that: '... the passage of time has distanced us from the evidence and the possibility of distinguishing guilt from innocence ...'
>
> Today's announcement is a significant step towards recognizing that all these men were victims of war, and it is certainly appropriate and poignant in this year of the 90th Anniversary of the Battle of the Somme.[15]

At the end of the memorandum is printed the Legion's mission statement in respect of the subject:

> The Legion has long supported the efforts of the campaigners and has included members of the Shot at Dawn Campaign in the Cenotaph Parade on Remembrance Sunday. We also facilitate a memorial plot at our National Memorial Arboretum in Alrewas, [Litchfield] Staffordshire.[16]

The Glynneath Town Council readily agreed to engrave Private William Jones' name on its war memorial – it was certainly one of the first to do so – and following the inclusion of his name organised a dedication ceremony, which was followed by a reception.

Private Thomas Henry Basil Rigby

11490 Private Thomas Henry (known as Harry) Basil Rigby, 10th Battalion South Wales Borderers, was a regular soldier who had joined up when he was 18 years of age in February 1914. He was probably a Lancastrian.

He had been sent to France in the September of 1915, nearly a week after his marriage. He was a brigade runner on the front line when he absconded from the recently captured enemy trenches on the Ypres Salient in August 1917. He was a recidivist, already serving a three-year suspended sentence for desertion.

He was arrested in Calais – his aim was probably to get across the Channel back to England – by a lance-corporal of the military police. He was still wearing his uniform but without cap or shoulder badges and initially gave a false name and pretended that he was a member of the staff at a camp based at Boulogne. He spent a day in custody before giving his true identity.

At the time he absconded as many as fifty members of his battalion, following the attack on the German lines, had to be evacuated with shell shock. He was possibly suffering from it too, but no mention was made of it during his trial. There he said he had deserted because he was worried about his wife's health.

He was executed at Armentières on 22 November 1917 and his body buried in Cite Bonjean Military Cemetery. He was 21 years of age.

Private William Scholes

44174 Private William Scholes, 2nd Battalion South Wales Borderers, was a conscript born in 1893. He became the last man serving in a Welsh regiment to be executed for desertion or any other offence during the war.

Ernest Thurtle made reference to this soldier in his publication *Shootings at Dawn*, using material that had been forwarded to him in a letter that stated that the soldier was not a coward and a braver man never went on active service. Yet Scholes was a recidivist who was serving a suspended sentence when he decided to abscond for a second time. The reasons for his flight seem to be because of his concern for his widowed mother not receiving an adequate fiscal allowance. This argument would never carry any weight in a trial and he was condemned to death.

He was executed on 10 August 1918, just over three months before the end of the war. He was 25 years of age and his body is buried in Borre Cemetery.

Chapter Five

The Edwin Dyett
Case

In February 1918 the editor of the popular *John Bull* magazine, Horatio Bottomley, wrote and article entitled 'Shot at Dawn':

> I have often pleaded the cause of Tommy. I want to plead that of the young officer – the mere boy – who at his country's call left his profession, his university, his home, to take command – as he well knew at the risk of his life – over those who, content with the role of private, had also rallied to the colours.[17]

This was regarding the case of Sub-Lieutenant Edwin Leopold Arthur Dyett of Albany Road, Cardiff.

Unlike many of the court martials involving shot at dawn cases, we are fortunate that the trial papers are, mostly, intact and that we can see the whole scenario.

Edwin Dyett was born on 17 October 1895 into a family with an impressive military background. His father was a captain in the Merchant Navy and later in the war was to serve as chief naval transport officer at Liverpool Naval Base. On his paternal side he was related to Sir John French, Commander in Chief at the outbreak of the hostilities. Both his grandfathers had been colonels who became Military Knights of Windsor and another member of the family, on his maternal side, had served in the Indian Mutiny of Lucknow.

Dyett enlisted in the Royal Naval Voluntary Reserve in June 1915. His preference was to be in the ranks but the preferred method in the services at that time was promoting men from military or aristocratic backgrounds into positions of authority. This philosophy, common in many countries, was that they would make good and efficient leaders of men because of their excellent backgrounds and education. Thus Edwin Dyett was made a commissioned officer – a sub-lieutenant because of his family history and not, like many of his class, from displaying a proven record in leading men.

He was commissioned into the Royal Naval (RN) Infantry Division – not his choice; he would have preferred to go to sea as a Royal Navy officer. The RN Division was created by Winston Churchill in 1914 to protect Antwerp and the channel ports, but by 1915 it had seen action in the Gallipoli Expedition. This ill-fated foray accounted for many lives, including the poet Rupert Brooke, who was bitten and killed by an infected mosquito. By the summer of 1916 the division had been directed to France to swell the numbers of the infantry on the Western Front. Thus, together with other RN Division officers, Edwin Dyett found himself in the trenches alongside members of the army instead of tasting the salty atmosphere of the world's oceans.

By the autumn of 1916 the Somme Offensive had become literally a war of attrition; trench warfare at its worst. The weather had changed and the rain turned everything into a smelly quagmire of mud, rats and dead British and German soldiers. It is on record that Dyett had requested to be sent back to sea because 'his nerves couldn't stand the strain of trench warfare'.

The Nelson Division, of which Dyett was an officer, lost its commanding officer, General Paris, who was badly wounded in October when fighting in the front line. The often-mooted argument that generals fought the war from cosy offices at HQ well behind the lines is dispelled by General Paris' experience. In total during the Great War, 224 generals were killed or wounded whilst physically taking part in the conflict.

The army's response to the loss of RN Division's General Paris was to replace him with Major General Shute. The enmity that clearly existed between the infantry and RN Division would be solved when Shute sorted them out.

The beginning of Edwin Dyett's downfall started when RN Division was detailed to attack north of the Ancre against established German lines; many in the ranks of the RN Division saw this as an opportunity to show the army how well they could fight. After the advance had started, the Nelson Battalion was kept in reserve – a ploy to feed men into the advancing party as they fell, to replenish their numbers. The attack broke down and was overrun by the bombardment of the German artillery, although two leading battalions had a degree of initial success by overrunning the Germans and taking hundreds prisoner.

Those Germans who had been bypassed in their trenches and bunkers turned the machine guns on the naval infantry-men milling around in the mist. Machine gun bullets blew everything in their path into the air, including mud, wood and naval 'soldiers'.

Chaos reigned as unseen aggressors fired bullets into the attackers running into the mist and then pinning down the second wave. They were shot to bits. However, two of the leading battalions experienced more measurable success and runners returned with information that there had been hundreds of naval casualties but, despite this and the hardships of a lack of ammunition, German and front-line trenches were now in British hands.

Edwin Dyett had not been involved in this attack. His Nelson Battalion having been in reserve, the Brigade Commander ordered the two officers, one of whom was Dyett, to advance to the front line to see exactly what was happening.

Both officers reported to the Advance Brigade HQ, waiting for instructions before being told to move up. Dyett writes to a friend about the scene:

> There was considerable hostile artillery, gas shells and tear shells falling all around us, and snipers were all over the place; we had very narrow shaves, more than once. We couldn't find our unit and rambled about.

As darkness fell the two officers failed to find their units in the hindering mud and fog. They decided to separate and search alone. Dyett came upon Sub-Lieutenant John Herring, who was organising fellow stragglers to return to the front. Herring was junior to Dyett, but nevertheless he ordered Dyett to join the column and return to the front to make sure that no one fell out.

Dyett refused and an argument between them broke out, which concluded with Dyett choosing to return to Brigade HQ for fresh orders. Herring sent back an order to HQ stating that Dyett had refused a lawful order. Enroute to HQ, Dyett came across men from 'A' Company and together in the dark and the confusion, they took refuge in a dugout.

The carnage and confusion of the attack is summed up in the following extract by W.E. Bland, of the Neslon Battalion:

> Our second in command was there, had the good fortune to say, 'I think you will find the safest way is up by the railway.' The road and the river ran parallel at that point. Because on the other side was a redoubt which was holding out and it turned out afterwards that it accounted for one of our sections,

completely wiped them out. We made our way and we came to what I think was known as the yellow line, which was our objective and established our guns. Our men were all dead tired, so tired they were falling asleep. And all the time we were anticipating a counter attack by the Germans from Beaumont Hamel, which fortunately never developed.

Shortly after that, I cannot remember why, I was sent off to find the Brigade major for further instructions. And it was whilst I was on the road that a high explosive came over and hit the road close by, which put an end to my active service. [The explosion caused Bland damage to his face, including his eye.]

A terrific trumpeting went on in my head. And I thought to myself, is this being killed?

I remember very little until my Petty Officer, Wallace Denleigh, said, 'Come on I will help you to the Dressing Station.' I had got various wounds. I had fractured a clavicle and had numerous flesh wounds on the right hand side of my body. These were attended to and I was put on a stretcher and carried by four German prisoners down to a line of waiting ambulances.[18]

Sub-Lieutenant R.B. Rackham of Hawke Battalion also gave an account:

It was a terrible day for the Hawke Battalion which in the early stages was devastated. I should say within 20 minutes of the opening of the battle the Hawke Battalion as a fighting force almost ceased to exist.

I didn't go over in the first line; I came over in a later line and there was a German strong point, which had not been dealt with by the gunners or the leading troops. And one could see the Germans there. Actually I saw one shooting at me, and I dropped down and unfortunately my batman, behind me, caught it, falling on me and died on me, as a result. We couldn't do much all that day but the following day two tanks were sent up and various maneuvers (I think the Germans were so frightened of the tanks) they simply surrendered and this strong point was mopped up. But it had done amazing damage against the battalions that had come up against it.

It was very elaborate. The machine guns were on lifts, down in the dugout and were simply lifted up and came into position on top. I would think there were half a dozen machine guns in that strong point, an area of about a circular 100 yards. The Ancre area slopes down quite steeply and then up the other side to Thiepval. We were just on the level, as it were, and that is where this strong point was and devastated both the Hawke and Nelson Battalions. It didn't rise above ground level. The machine guns came up and its crew mounted on these lifts by manual means, a winding handle used by people below. As a result the Battalion below was very badly mauled. But those on the slopes and down to the river, mainly the Hood and the Hawke, were most successful. The strong point didn't really cover that area for two reasons, one because they were shielded from it, and secondly because of the amazing leadership given to the Hood by Colonel Freyberg, which resulted in his VC.

During the night, what were called our first reinforcements, which were left behind, came up and joined us. So we had other officers, among whom was the Assistant Adjutant, one A.P. Herbert. He came and joined me with our little band, I think we had only 30 or 40 men left.

This last segment of the attack involving the Nelson Battalion, of which Dyett was held in reserve took a mauling. Hundreds of men were killed. A 189th Infantry Brigade report of the fighting records:

Nelson Battalion advanced close up on the barrage and suffered considerably from our own artillery fire. Still the last two lines advanced and, keeping in touch with the barrage, arrived

at the steep bank, situated between the German third line and
Station Road, known as the Terraces. They met considerable
opposition, but, after hand to hand fighting with bombs and
bayonet, the remainder advanced to Station Road. Dugouts
here were cleared with little opposition and the advance continued to the green line with difficulty.

Meanwhile the 3rd and 4th waves encountered very heavy
sustained machine gun fire and suffered very heavy casualties and
lost cohesion and direction and, except for small detached parties,
ceased to exist as a fighting force. Battalion HQ passed the
original front line at about 6.30 a.m. and advanced into no man's
land, but then came under very heavy fire itself, from close range.
It afterwards transpired that a proportion of the German front
line system was still holding out in a stronghold. In front of this
the Nelson's Commanding Officer and Adjutant were both killed.
This strong point was holding up a large number of troops from
all battalions by its heavy machine gun fire. Therefore the RND
men began to dig in and at this time Lieutenant Dangerfield,
the Nelson's Signal Officer, did excellent work in rallying parties
of men who had lost their officers, in an endeavour to organize
an attack against the strong point. He also ran a line to the HQ of
his Battalion, although slightly wounded in the hand.[19]

The above illustrates the conflict that the Nelson Battalion,
together with others, had been involved in and that the battalion had incurred huge casualties. Dyett had been on the
periphery of this, used as a reinforcement. The problem
arose when Herring issued him with an order which Dyett felt
unable to accept. He moved back to his HQ to obtain, as he
said, further orders. He was reported for refusing the order,
which activated the court martial.

The fact that Herring and Dyett had some sort of history
didn't help the latter's case. Dyett says in a letter that Herring
'was my one and only enemy': it is stated that Dyett had

reported or chastised Herring some months earlier for taking a woman back to his billet.

Contrary to many of the cases involving field court martials and general court martials, Dyett's, by the measures and conditions in the field, certainly was not a rushed affair. He waited, whilst under close arrest, from 15 November to 19 December before he knew that his case was being proceeded with. He seemed convinced that a hearing would not be held.

On 13 December he writes to a friend:

> We went up the line and took over the right sector for four days; there we were relieved and returned to our billets, and my Company, with others, during the night took up our positions, and things went fairly well until late in the morning, when I was detailed to go and replace casualties – you were in that scrap, so there is no need to explain how many. I crossed no man's land later in the afternoon, but could not find a man belonging to my unit. My companion went off with a crowd we met, but as I still held hope of finding the Company, I rambled about and lost touch with everybody, and my nerves, not being strong were completely strung up. I met another officer, who says he ordered me to join up with another party, but this I did not do, but wandered about still looking for my own unit. In the meantime this gentleman went back and sent a startling message of sorts to BHQ, with result that they are trying to kick me out of it, but up to now the evidence is not strong enough to cause a 'sitting'. And that is what happened to me in the biggest advance – luck, isn't it? It makes me sick to think of it, and they have now kept me a month hanging on. I am hoping for news any day now, and if there is nothing in it do not see why I should worry my people by telling them. Now I have all the Company's letters to censor, so please excuse more.[20]

No news had been made known to him by Christmas Eve about the case proceeding. Despite being under close arrest he seems to still be engaged in the battalion's work, carrying out administrative duties by censoring mail, and he elaborates further:

I hear that you are still worrying about me more than is necessary. I will explain my present situation so as to relieve your mind. I was surplus, and was sent off at five minutes' notice I went up with another officer of my Battalion who was senior by one ring. We reported ourselves at Brigade Headquarters as instructed by our Lieutenant-in-Command. At that time they had lost touch with the Battalion, so we awaited an hour or so in the dugouts awaiting orders, which we got – at least, the other man got them, and then after a lot of trouble I got them to tell me what they were and we proceeded towards Boche overland ...

When it was dark we met a body of men with an officer in charge; they were wanted by Colonel Freyberg VC Hood Battalion; there was much confusion and disorder going on, and my nerves became strung up to the highest extreme. I found that my companion had gone off somewhere with the men. The officer who was leading the party we met was my 'one and only enemy', so we were not polite to each other, and as he is junior to me I practically ignored him except for telling him I was going back to BHQ, which I had left and hour or two before in daylight, but finding those places was not as easy a matter as I thought, with the result that I got lost for the second time. I found an NCO of the old A Company – we rambled about until he fell down for want of sleep, but I managed to get him along. Later my voice was recognized by some more men of the A Company who were lost; they attached themselves to me, saying they also were looking for BH Quarters. BHQ however was not to be found that night. My nerves were completely gone and my head was singing. About then we came across a funk hole, and there we stayed. However my 'enemy' had gone back behind his supports and sent a startling message to BHQ concerning me. I have been under close arrest ever since November 14th.

On November 8th I put in an application to the Commanding Officer telling him my reasons for wanting to return to sea on account of my nerves not being able to stand the strain. He told me he was just the same as I, so I let it slide at that, as I didn't want anyone to say that I was trying to 'swing the lead' as others have done. I have obeyed orders, and that is all I care about it. Things are very one sided just now, but as soon as I have my little say in the matter it will alter their colour altogether. Now that is as much as you can know of what happened as you have found out for yourself.'[21]

In this letter he expresses both a degree of optimism and some pessimism regarding the situation he finds himself in. Yet the charge papers had been drawn up on 19 December and his trial was held on Boxing Day. He was charged on two counts.

The First Charge: The accused, Temporary Sub-Lieutenant Edwin Leopold Arthur Dyett RNVR, an officer of the Nelson Battalion 63rd Division, is charged when on active service deserting His Majesty's Service

In that he

In the field on the 13th November 1916, when it was his duty to join his battalion, which was engaged in operations against the Enemy, did not do so, and remained absent from his battalion until placed under arrest at Englebelmer on the 15th November 1916.

Alternative Charge: Conduct to the prejudice of good order and Military discipline

In that he

In the field on the 13th November 1916 did not go up to the front line when it was his duty to do so.[22]

Dyett's trial opened on the morning of the 26 December. He pleaded not guilty to both charges. Among those hearing the case and acting as judge advocate was another Welshman, Captain J.S. Griffith-Jones of the 10th Battalion, South Wales Borderers, who had been a barrister before the war.

The case was prosecuted by Sub-Lieutenant Herbert Slade Strickland of Nelson Battalion and Dyett was defended by Sub Lieutenant Cecil Cameron Travanion of the Hawke Battalion, who had qualified as a solicitor a year or so before the outbreak of the war.

Lieutenant Commander E.W. Nelson of the Nelson Battalion was the first officer presented by the prosecution:

> On 13 November, 1916, I was in command of the officers of the Nelson Battalion who were not taken into action with the Battalion at the commencement of the operations. We were then stationed at Hedauville. In RN Divisional Headquarters I detailed Lieutenant Truscott and the accused to report to Brigade Headquarters. I personally gave these orders to both these officers and told them that a car was waiting to take them up to Divisional Headquarters.
>
> I saw both these officers leave in this car. The accused appeared to be quite nervous when I gave him these orders.[23]

Under cross-examination, Nelson added that in his opinion the accused's ability as an officer was very poor. He added that his authority to command men was not good and confirmed that the accused had written to him asking to be sent back to sea. He concluded by saying that he had more confidence in the abilities of Truscott than he had in that of the accused.

The second witness for the prosecution was Lieutenant Cyril Alfred Truscott, Nelson Battalion.

On 13th November 1916, I received orders from Lieutenant Commander Nelson. In compliance with these orders I joined the accused at Divisional HQ and drove the car towards Brigade Headquarters. Brigade HQ was at that time in a trench called Charles Street, between the villages of Mesnil and Hamel.

On our arrival at Brigade HQ I went into the HQ dugout while the accused remained just outside it ...

I there received certain orders from Brigadier-General L.F. Phillips, which I communicated to the accused. I told the accused 'that the Brigadier has said that we were to go and join the Battalion which had last been heard of in the Green Line'. Green Line is represented on the map I now produce by the blue pencil line.[24]

The map was signed by the president and attached to the statement.

Truscott continued:

I showed the accused the position of Green Line on my map as we were going up to join the Battalion in compliance with Brigadier-General Phillip's orders.

At Beaucourt Station the accused and I met a large number of men following Lieutenant Herring up the road. The accused and Lieutenant Herring entered into a heated conversation.

I proceeded to make enquires for my Battalion from men of the party and particularly asked if any of my own Battalion were present among them.

On finding twenty-five men of my own Battalion I took charge of them and marched them towards the Green Line. I left the accused still arguing with Lieutenant Herring.

Lieutenant Herring was not an officer in our Battalion and I did not know him.

I gave the accused no orders for he belonged to another Company and I thought we should each be going to our respective Companies. I therefore left him.

I did not hear any of the conversation between the accused and Lieutenant Herring.

I did not see the accused again until about mid-day on 15 November at Englebelmer.

The accused appeared to be normal when he was with me on 13 November. I noticed nothing strange in his demeanour.

It was about 5.45 p.m. when I saw the accused.[25]

Under cross-examination, Truscott said that he saw no sign of 'cold feet' or any indication that the accused was going to desert. He confirmed that he had not given the accused any orders and had merely passed on the communication, the brigadier general's orders, to him.

Sub-Lieutenant John Leigh Herring was the fifth witness to give evidence for the prosecution. He was attached to Drake Battalion, RND:

On 13 November last I was attached to the 189th Brigade Headquarters. I was in charge of the ammunition supply at Hamel, where I had my dumps. I was responsible that the ammunition was sent up from these to the firing line.

About 4.30 p.m. or 5 p.m. I saw the accused and Sub Lieutenant Truscott at Beaucourt Station.

I knew the accused before, as I came out from England in the same draft as him.

Just before Lieutenant Truscott and the accused came up I had taken charge of 200 men, whom I found to be retiring. I ordered them to 'about turn'. I made back towards the firing line. I realised that these men had no business to be retiring.

When Lieutenant Truscott came up to me and inquired for his Battalion I told him to take charge of the 200 men and to take them back to the firing line with him. I gave this order and an order and he took the majority of the party off to the left.

I then saw the accused and said to him: 'You go in the rear of those men and follow Truscott.'

The accused then replied: 'I am not the senior officer and I find such chaos here. I think I had better go back and report to the Brigade.'

I then went back to Hamel Dump and I noticed that the accused followed me. On arrival at my dump I at once wrote a message concerning the accused to the Staff Captain.

I did not see the accused until I got back to Arqueves about 15 November.

At the time that the accused and Truscott came up to me there was some confusion owing to the retirement of these men without an officer and there was a certain amount of shelling of the road going on. There was no attack actually proceeding at the time.

Accused appeared as if he expected to find his Battalion and he expected to report to his Battalion. The accused did not seem to grasp the situation. He was not agitated or frightened.

When I told the accused to follow Lieutenant Truscott, he appeared to resent it. He told me he was going to report at Brigade HQ, that he knew where the HQ was as he had just come from there.[26]

About halfway in the script on the court martial file are the words written in pencil: 'In the Navy does a Sub-Lt give orders to a Lt?'

Under cross-examination by Dyett's counsel, Herring said:

I was engaged on the Headquarters Staff and therefore I felt myself justified in ordering Lieutenant Truscott and the accused. Under the circumstances I felt myself justified in giving the order, though my particular and special duty had reference to communications and information only.

Had Lieutenant Truscott behaved in the same manner as the accused did, I would have reported him.[27]

Dyett's counsel clarifies the point: 'Had Lieutenant Truscott disobeyed your order, would you have reported him?'

Herring answered by saying, 'Yes, under the circumstances I consider I had authority to order my senior officer.'

Herring was asked about his own relationship with the accused. He replied by saying that he had no personal animosity against the officer.

He was asked why there had been an altercation between them. Herring said that he (Dyett) appeared to resent his giving him an order.

The prosecutor then re-examined Herring clearly, to clarify his statement that he would have reported Truscott if he had disobeyed his order, an order given to a senior officer.

Herring said: 'I certainly should have reported Lieutenant Truscott if he had left the men where they were and followed me back.'

An acting petty officer was called to give evidence for the prosecution. This witness claimed to have been privy to part of the altercation which did take place between Sub-lieutenant Herring and Sub-lieutenant Dyett.

His evidence reads:

On 13 November I accompanied Sub Lieutenant Herring as his assistant. I remember seeing Lieutenant Herring and the accused talking to each other near Beaucourt Station.

I overheard Lieutenant Herring tell Lieutenant Truscott, who was also present to take charge of about 200 men and take them up to the firing line. I also heard Lieutenant Herring tell the accused, who was with Lieutenant Truscott 'to give Lieutenant Truscott a hand with some of the men'. I cannot remember the exact words used but I have related the effect.

The accused did not carry out Lieutenant's Herring's instructions. He turned to Lieutenant Herring and said, 'I cannot take charge among all this chaos and disorder. I will return to Brigade for orders.'

I next saw the accused turn in the direction of Brigade Headquarters. I last saw him in Hamel Dump.

The accused did not appear to grasp the situation when Lieutenant Herring told him to go with Lieutenant Truscott.[28]

When cross-examined by the defence counsel, the acting petty officer (his actual name cannot be identified on the record) reiterated the accusation that Dyett seemed to resent taking an order from Lt Herring.

Then he added the following damning opinion:

[The] accused did not look as if he was afraid or in funk. He looked as if he wanted to get out of it.[29]

On the record this last remark is underlined in red.

There were eight witnesses called for the prosecution: Lieutenant Commander E.W. Nelson, Nelson Battalion; Lieutenant C.A. Truscott, Nelson Battalion; Brigadier General Lewis Francis Phillips, General Officer Commanding 189th Infantry Brigade; Captain A.R. Bare, Staff Captain, 189th Brigade (RN) Division; Sub-Lieutenant John Leigh Herring, Drake Battalion, RND; Sub-Lieutenant E.V.G. Gardner, Nelson Battalion; an acting petty officer [the name is unclear on the file]; and Lieutenant Bernard Dangerfield, Nelson Battalion.

Most of the witness statements are repetitive, differing in only minor details. After the last witness, Lieutenant Dangerfield, gave his evidence the case for the prosecution was complete.

The court did not seek clarification on points that had been made. Only Herring's version of the reasons for the altercation between himself and Dyett is recorded; and the defence solicitor didn't challenge the petty officer when he gave his opinion that the accused 'looked as if he wanted to get out of it'. No other witness opined anything like this. Nor did the defence solicitor challenge the petty officer regarding collusion in the making of the witness statement: an identical sentence appears in both Herring's and the petty officer's statement: 'He didn't appear to grasp the situation.'

The court no doubt felt any questions it might have had would be addressed when Dyett gave evidence on his own behalf. It was probably amazed and surprised when no defence was made by the Welshman.

The court's president, Brigade S.F. Metcalfe, asked Dyett: Do you apply to give evidence yourself as a witness?

Dyett's reply: 'No.'

The president asked: 'Do you intend to call any other witnesses in your defence?'

Dyett said: 'No.'

The president asked: 'Have you anything to say in your defence?'

Dyett said: 'I do not wish to say anything at all.'

One wonders, by reading Dyett's letters written between 13 November and the period leading up to the trial, if he still believed 'there is nothing in it'. When one of the witnesses, a junior in rank to him, had said, 'he looked like he wanted to get out of it', one would have thought that Dyett would have wanted to give evidence and challenge this opinion – because that is all it was and not a factual statement that could be substantiated. Indeed, other witnesses said that they did not think that Dyett's action of refusing the order issued by Herring, and making his way back to headquarters, was an act of a man deserting. We have no means of knowing whether his defence solicitor tried to advise Dyett to defend himself or if, through Dyett's ignorance of the procedures of the Army Act under which the trial was conducted – and it was properly conducted – he had been advised to offer a defence and had refused. He would have known the possible consequences of being found guilty of desertion. Dyett's future was to be decided on the prosecution case only.

The prosecutor addressed the court:

> I had not intended to say anything at all. Having regard, however, to the evidence that has been adduced, I should like to point out that, even if the accused did not receive any direct orders to go up to join his Battalion, it was his duty to do so under the circumstances he found to be existing on his arrival at Beaucourt Station.[30]

Sub-Lieutenant Cecil Trevanion addressed the court for the defence, drawing attention to Dyett's nervous disposition and that he had made the request to be returned to the navy. He stressed that he believed that the accused and Lieutenant Truscott would have continued to make a direct advance to the Green Line in search of their battalions and that Sub-Lieutenant Herring's instructions confused the situation.

He pointed out that both the petty officer and Sub-Lieutenant Herring had admitted that the accused was not showing signs of fear and both their statements had used the identical phrase that 'he seemed unable to grasp the situation'.

Trevanion, clearly doing his best to address the charge of desertion, argued that Dyett had got lost on his way to HQ and had, with others, spent the night in a dugout and then reported at Englebelmer and Lieutenant Commander Egerton RNVR, who had asked him if he was going to HQ. He had answered saying he would wait for his battalion.

Trevanion rightly stressed to the court that the charge of desertion had no support from any of the prosecution witnesses.

He agreed that the accused had shown little initiative in not grasping the new instruction and his return to HQ was for further orders.

Reading Travanion's submission, in view of the fact that Dyett was not going to offer a defence, it is spirited and accurate. He did the best he could have.

Captain J.S. Griffith-Jones, the judge advocate, summed up the charge of desertion using *The Manual of Military Law*:

> In respect to the Alternative Charge of Conduct to the prejudice of good order and Military Discipline the Court would use its military knowledge to determine if the acts referenced in the charges, if proved would account to conduct as was prejudicial to both military discipline and good order.[31]

Captain Griffith-Jones, addressing the submitted evidence regarding the first charge, noted that no medical evidence had been requested and pointed out that the accused had not reported to the staff captain, brigade HQ or the general. He was absent throughout 14 November and was next seen on 15 November. Captain Griffith-Jones said that the court must be satisfied regarding 'intention', that mistake or error of judgment did not amount to intent.

And that was it. The court martial of Sub-Lieutenant Edwin Dyett of Cardiff was over.

The announcement was made that:

> The Court find that the accused, Temporary Sub-Lieutenant Edwin Leopold Arthur Dyett RNVR, an officer of the Nelson Battalion, 63rd Division is Guilty of the First Charge but Not Guilty of the Alternative Charge.[32]

The court then reconvened to receive information regarding details of the character and conduct of Dyett. Lieutenant

Dangerfield, Acting Adjutant of Nelson Battalion, provided the details, which, once given, were not cross-examined by the defence solicitor.

The court announced the sentence: temporary Sub-Lieutenant Edwin Leopold Arthur Dyett RNVR, an officer of the Nelson Battalion, 63rd Division, was to suffer death by being shot. It did make a recommendation for mercy:

> That he is very young and has no experience of active operations of this nature. And that the circumstances of growing darkness, heavy shelling and the fact that men were retiring in considerable numbers were likely to affect seriously a youth, unless he had a strong character.[33]

The documents were signed at 'Champneuf, France this Twenty-Sixth Day of December 1916'.

The documentation of the court martial was sent to the deputy judge advocate general and on to the adjutant general for the legality of the trial to be approved by 28 December 1916. Once approved it was forwarded to the Fifth Army.

On 28 December, Assistant Adjutant General (AAG) for the Adjutant Colonel wrote: 'Will you please forward your recommendations as to whether the sentence should be carried out or commuted and those of the Divisional and Corps Commander.'

Major General C.D. Shute, Commander, 63rd (RN) Division wrote:

> The Division did very well on the Ancre and behaved most gallantly. Added to this Sub Lieutenant Dyett is very young and inexperienced. Beyond the above I know of no reason why the extreme penalty should not be exacted.
>
> I recommend mercy.[34]

On 30 December 1916, Lieutenant General C.M. Macob, Commander V Corps wrote:

> I see no reason why the sentence should not be carried out.[35]

On 31 December General H. Gough, Commander Fifth Army, wrote:

> I recommend that the sentence be carried out. If a private had behaved as he did in such circumstances, it is highly probable that he would be shot.[36]

On 2 January 1917, Field Marshal Douglas Haig confirmed the sentence. Dyett's fate was sealed.

Julian Putkowski and Julian Sykes in *Shot at Dawn* make a further important point of Dyett's status in the navy:

> Under Naval Law a sentence of death could not be carried out without the sanction of the Admiralty. And whilst there is no doubt that Dyett was also subject to the Army Act there is no reason to believe that any consideration was given to this additional requirement. There is little doubt that the consent of the 'Senior Service' was never obtained, nor would it have been given. Dyett may not only have been shot unjustly, but also illegally.[37]

Sometime on 4 January 1917, Edwin Dyett was playing cards with two battalion officers when another officer entered the building and read out his death warrant – he was to be shot at dawn the following morning. A padre was present and spent some time with him so he could be at peace with God. He had the strength of mind to write to his mother:

> Dearest Mother Mine, I hope by now you will have heard the news. Dearest, I am leaving you now because He has

willed it. My sorrow tonight is for the trouble I have caused you and dad.

Please excuse any mistakes, but if it were not for the kind support of the rev. W.C ... who is with me tonight, I should not be able to write myself. I should like you to write to him as he has been my friend.

I am leaving all my effects to you, dearest; will you give my little ... half the sum you have of mine?

Give dear dad my love and wish him luck. I feel for you so much and I am sorry for bringing dishonour upon you all. Give ... my love. She will, I expect, understand – and give her back the presents, photos, cards, etc., she has sent me, poor girl.

So now dearest Mother, I must close. May God bless and protect you all now and for evermore. Amen.[38]

Edwin Dyett was led out as dawn slowly illuminated the French landscape a few minutes before 7.30 a.m. at St Firmin. Tied to a post, blindfolded and with a piece of white cloth placed over his heart, by 7.30 a.m. he was dead. He was 21 years of age and his body was buried in Le Crotoy Communal Cemetery.

An eyewitness account of the execution scene was published in *John Bull* magazine on 23 February 1918:

Can you picture that final scene? The prisoner tied to a stake; there was no need – he faced death fearlessly, but the cords cut him and he protested – his eyes bandaged, his identification disc suspended just over his left breast. The firing party, half hidden in a trench. No time is wasted. And yet there comes the cry: 'For God's sake put me out of my misery – this suspense is killing me.' And, as the rifles made their first click, 'Well, boys, goodbye. For God's sake, shoot straight.' And this from one who stood there and saw it all: 'He was no coward; he behaved like a pukka white man.' And this from the lad himself, in that dread hour: 'Yes I can face this, but I couldn't face the Boche.'[39]

And from Leeds University's *Liddle Collection*, a taped recollection by J. Blacklock of the Nelson Battalion taped in June 1971:

> I got off it, got out of being on the firing squad. I said to the Petty Officer, 'I will never sleep well if I shot one of our own.' He refers specifically to Dyett: 'He told them to shoot straight, that's what he said!'[10]

And published in *John Bull* magazine on 23 February 1918, the letter the padre wrote to Dyett's mother after the event:

> I enclose your boy's last letter to his mother. I want you to understand he wrote it entirely by himself, his mind being as clear and thoughtful as anyone could wish; not a tremor or a moment of fear. When his end had been carried out, I accompanied his body in an ambulance car several miles away to a beautiful little cemetery, near a small town, quite close to the sea, and here we buried him with a Church of England Service. A cross will soon be erected over his grave. Leave it to me, and I will see that it is done, before our hurried departure to another part of France.[11]

In his book, *For God's Sake Shoot Straight*, Leonard Sellers quotes Ernest Thurtle. This Labour MP had campaigned against the execution of servicemen in *Military Discipline and Democracy* and relates the following:

> In July 1919 a gallant infantry officer, Colonel Lambert Ward, appealed in the House of Commons against any differentiation between the graves of those who had been killed in action, or had died of wounds and sickness, and those unfortunate men who had been shot for cowardice or desertion. In the midst of a painful silence that could be felt he spoke as follows:

'I ask the House not to dismiss this petition with the remark that these men were cowards and deserved their fate. They were not cowards in the accepted meaning of the word. At any rate they did not display one-tenth part of the cowardice that was displayed by the crowds in London who went flocking to the Tube Stations on the first alarm of an air raid. These men, many of them, volunteered in the early days of the war to serve their country. They tried and they failed.

'I think that it is well that it should be made publicly known and that the people of this country should understand ... that from the point of view of Tommy up in the trenches, war is not a question of honours and decorations, but war is just hell ...'

In uttering these words, the soldier was lifting a corner of the veil of make-believe which hides from the public the real feelings of the actual fighting men of an army.[12]

In the Imperial War Museum's Department of Documents, the clerk to the 189th Brigade, Thomas MacMillan wrote:

Without going out of my way I leaned that the unfortunate officer had waited so long for the verdict to be promulgated that he and his guard held the strong belief that he would be given the chance to redeem himself. He was actually playing cards with two officers when the fatal news was communicated to him and he was given only a few hours to prepare for death.

Some days after the shooting a bulky package arrived at Brigade Headquarters and I found it contained all the papers bearing on the trial. I had only time to glance over them when I was summoned to the mess, and I had no option but to take the papers with me. That was the last I saw of them, but my hasty perusal sufficed to disclose who the witnesses for the prosecution were, and from that moment I resolved to shun them both, for one of them was none other than the Petty Officer who shaped so badly on the Peninsula and the other an officer for whom I had a very poor regard.

I had also observed that, although the young officer had been found guilty, there was a strong recommendation to mercy, and in common with others I wondered what consideration had been given to the recommendation.

Was he, I wondered, to be the first martyr to the clamour from the ranks for an example to be made of an officer for desertion of cowardice? How many officers have been guilty of this offence, and why have they not been made to answer for it with their lives, as we have to do? The higher Command must have heard this grouse grow louder and could not fail to admit the justice of it.

If, however, they were forced to act, why did they select a mere boy for their first victim? It was obvious that the lad had been commissioned to control men before he had learned to control himself. Surely there were senior officers who had been guilty of desertion or cowardice – officers whose age, experience and responsibility made their crime so much more reprehensible.

The unfortunate youth had been well represented at his trial by a fellow officer who was a qualified solicitor. As there was a fair proportion of men with legal training in fighting units, some horrible individual, far removed from the danger zone conceived the sinister plan of withdrawing all such and attaching them to the Judge advocate's department, and soon this was given effect to.

Many left to join the circus, but this officer who acted as a Prisoner's Friend in the case in question carried on with his soldiering and, if he had not all his wits about him, he might have paid dearly for the part he played at the trial.[13]

The above serves to illustrate the attitude of some senior officers at the time towards those who acted as prisoner's friend at these hearings. Many soldiers who were condemned to death were not represented but Dyett was, by a qualified solicitor. Thomas MacMillan writes on the subject again in respect of the Dyett case:

> The Battalion had been instructed to render a statement giving names of the officers who would participate in the next fight [in respect of the anticipated action at Garrelle] and as the lists arrived, I took them to the Major. His eagle eye observed that the officer who had acted as Prisoner's Friend [Sub-Lieutenant Cecil Cameron Trevanion] to the young man who was shot at dawn was on the reserve list. At this his monkey rose, and in his most unbearing manner he told me to instruct the Battalion Commander concerned to send the 'hard faced bastard forward'. But the young gent thus referred to knew all the tricks of his trade. On being informed of Brigade's intentions concerning him, he promptly developed a raging temperature and as promptly was evacuated to England.[44]

Edwin Dyett was literally written out of naval history following the action at Ancre on 13 November and the days following that date. Reports of the conflict make no mention of Dyett's execution.

In the years following the Great War, Edwin Dyett's father, Commander W.H.R. Dyett, carried on a campaign aided by the editor of the *John Bull* magazine, to try and get the findings overturned and get his son a pardon. This was, of course, unsuccessful despite certain reports to the contrary. Only in 2006 were posthumous pardons granted. His efforts were in vain and some years later he left Britain and settled in the USA.

Edwin Dyett was a victim of circumstances. When he, together with Truscott, embarked to the Green Line looking for their battalions, if they had not met Herring en route who complicated matters both officers would have undoubtedly continued searching for their men. Could the 21-year-old

Welshman from Cardiff just have been a suitable officer – a naval officer, for the army considered the naval division to be undisciplined – for the army to exact its wrath?

Dyett did not desert his position in the sense we understand: he refused to take an order, which was not even given to him directly, from a junior officer. When I visited the National Memorial Arboretum in the autumn of 2013 I asked a very senior officer if he would have, or was it the practice of custom to receive and accept orders from a junior officer? He looked astonished at the question. 'No, certainly not,' he said.

Edwin Dyett, rest your case. Rest in Peace.

Chapter Six

Executed for
Committing Murder

The soldiers who were executed for committing murder
were not subject to the blanket pardon that was granted
for other offences, excluding rape, although no solider was
executed for this offence in the Great War, committed under
the Army Act.

No one argued with this judgement, the general concerns
in respect of the Army Act were those offences that were
not punishable by death in civilian life; those found guilty of
murder and rape were liable to execution outside the theatre
of war until capital punishment was abolished in civilian life
in 1965. The last execution for rape in Great Britain was on
15 June 1945 when an American serviceman, Aniceto Martinez,
was hanged by Tom Pierrepoint and Albert Pierrepoint for
raping Agnes Cope in Rugeley, Staffordshire. He was executed
in Shepton Mallet.[15]

To have included the offence of murder in the 2006 blanket
pardon for soldiers would have caused ramifications in the
cases for every other execution in civilian life. Although, of
course, there is precedent for murder cases to be reviewed
and pardons posthumously granted many years later for

miscarriages of justice: Timothy Evans from Merthyr Vale was hanged at Pentonville by Albert Pierrepoint and Syd Dernley on 9 March 1950 – sixteen years later he was granted a Royal Pardon; Mahmood Hussain Mattan of Cardiff, hanged on 3 September 1952 by Albert Pierrepoint and Robert Stewart in Cardiff Prison, was granted a posthumous pardon after nearly forty-six years; and Derek Bentley, a 19 year old from London who was executed by Albert Pierrepoint and Harry Allen at Wandsworth Prison on 28 January 1953, was granted a pardon forty-five years later in 1998.

The span of time in these cases, which were very well documented, was forty-five/forty-six years. In the case of murderers in the Great War, a span of nearly 100 years is too cumbersome and only those advocates who oppose capital punishment in a historical sense would complain. The greater majority of those seeking justice for those men who were shot at dawn would accept that the Great War murderers, even when their cases could be argued they committed manslaughter, should be exempt from the blanket pardon.

In a Welsh context there were four soldiers shot for committing murder during the war: two from the Rhondda Valley; one from Pembrokeshire; and one whose town is unknown.

Private Richard Morgan and Lance Corporal William Price

11967 Private Richard Morgan and 12942 Lance Corporal William Price were both serving with the 2/Welsh Regiment and both from Rhondda. Aged 32 and 41 respectively, there appears to have been no evidence that they had been in trouble before this incident. They met their end in what became the fifth double execution of the war.

Both were experienced soldiers, as was their victim Company Sergeant Major Hugh Hayes, a veteran of the Boar War. The regiment had been carrying out work digging a second line of trenches near Bethune, working in the most appalling conditions, including snowfall. The two soldiers got drunk on the evening of 20 January 1915 and shot Company Sergeant Major Hugh Hayes.

Their trial, by general court martial, was held at Lillers on 6 February and both were found guilty of murder and sentenced to death. No consideration was given to the fact that they were drunk. Robert Graves, the poet, states in his 'Goodbye To All That' that Hayes had been accidentally shot. Other reports indicate the Hayes had been deliberately shot because he had been victimising the pair. Graves would have been writing retrospectively because he joined the battalion in the summer of that year.

The Reverend Harry Blackburne recounted in his book 'This Also Happened on the Western Front' that he had been with the men during the trial, that he read the parable of the Prodigal Son and prayed for them as they faced the firing squad. Their last words were: 'Stick it, the Welch'.

They were executed on 15 February 1915 and laid to rest in Bethune Town Cemetery, the same cemetery as their victim, Hugh Hayes. The town's cemetery register states that Hayes died of accidental injuries.[16]

Private Charles William Knight

15437 Private Charles William Knight was a 28-year-old Kitchener Volunteer from London, serving with the 10th Battalion of the Royal Welsh Fusiliers. His unit had been in France for a little less than a week and had been moved up to the front line within a few days when, on 3 November 1915, Knight entered his billet in a drunken state and started to shoot indiscriminately at members of his platoon. The result was that he killed Private Alfred Edwards and wounded another soldier. Company Sergeant Major Fisher promptly arrested him.

He was tried by field court martial three days later, which did not question that Knight had been very drunk and not acting in a responsible manner. The court would have considered whether Knight was in such a drunken stupor that he would not have realised what he was doing and found that he was not. His record would not have helped his cause: he had had five charges of drunkenness levied against him in just over a year and, to add to his woes, his commanding officer said:

> No 15437 Private Charles William Knight of the battalion under my command is a man of apparently very low origin, though of considerable personality. He had great influence amongst the other men, and was more than once recommended to me for promotion. He is a man who is addicted to drink, and when under its influence appears to lose control over his actions. He joined the BEF on 28th September last.

Even in this single statement the Commanding Officer Lieutenant Colonel Beresford-Ask has contradictions: a statement from his superior officer on the Western Front saying that Knight is apparently very low origin is damning, but then Beresford-Ask adds that 'he has considerable personality … and influence amongst the other men'. One can read into this that Knight's influence was for the good of the battalion. Also the court clearly rejected the penultimate sentence in the statement that 'he is a man who is addicted to drink and when under its influence appears to lose control over his actions'.

One asks why Beresford-Ask's opinion was not acted upon by the court. It is the one aspect of the statement that should have found him not guilty of murder. Yes, guilty of manslaughter, but that was not the charge.

Private Knight had no prisoner's friend to defend him. It is a lot to expect a man to keep his composure and coherently express himself in the heated atmosphere of a court martial, when his very life is in jeopardy. This requires the clearness of mind of a trained lawyer, not a soldier serving in the uncertain conditions of trench warfare.

The coal was added on to Knight's fire, which was burning out of control when, 'In my opinion,' said the commander of the 76th Brigade, 'it is a clear case of murder and owing to the ease of which men can obtain ammunition on active service it is necessary in such cases to carry out the extreme penalty of the law.'

Concern was expressed by Major General Haldene, who asked: 'Whether anyone else fired at all, or whether all the other rifles, being examined, showed no trace of being fired.'

The commander suggested:

> The finding not having been confirmed, it is possible to try the man again and bring out evidence on these points, should such a course of be considered necessary.
>
> There appears, however, to be no doubt that the accused's conduct was such that any 'reasonable man' must have known it was likely to cause grievous bodily harm, and that the charge is correct. I recommend that Private C. Knight's offence be treated as murder and not manslaughter.

The case hinged on the private's state of mind at the time of the offence with consideration as to whether, if he had not been in an inebriated state, he would have started firing his rifle in an indiscriminate fashion.

Lieutenant Colonel Beresford-Ask stated that the defendant was addicted to drink and when in that state was not in control of his actions.

Mayor Gilbert Mellor, when forwarding the trial documents to the adjutant general, wrote:

The substantial question for the Court to decide was whether the accused was in a state of mind to intend to kill or inflict grievous bodily harm or to know what he was doing would reasonably and probably cause the result, and in law it rested, in this case, upon the accused to show that he was not legally responsible for his actions.[17]

The crux of the entire scenario was the fact that Knight was not defended, which was the case in many of the courts martial held on the Western Front, no matter what the offence was. In this case – from the brief trial notes we have – there is little doubt that the soldier was very drunk and did not know what he was doing. Nevertheless, he was found guilty of murder (when it was probably manslaughter) and condemned to death. He was shot nine days later on 15 November 1915 and buried in Grand Hazard Military Cemetery.

Private James Skone

36224 Private James Skone was a Kitchener Volunteer from Pembroke attached to the 2/Welsh Regiment. The case of this solider mirrors the others, in that alcoholic drink was involved and made the man act irrationally. His record indicates that he was of good character, yet he had at the time of the shooting been placed under arrest for an absence from duty. It seems that this caused him to react by shooting Edwin Williams, a Lance Sergeant, on 13 April 1918 at Gorre, Bethune.

Private Skone was found guilty of murder and was shot on 10 May 1918 in Hersin, France. He was 39 years of age and a married man. His body is buried in Hersin Communal Cemetery Extension.

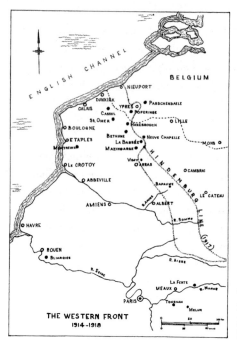

Two maps depicting the British Expeditionary Force on the Western Front 1914–18. (Artwork by Barrie Flint)

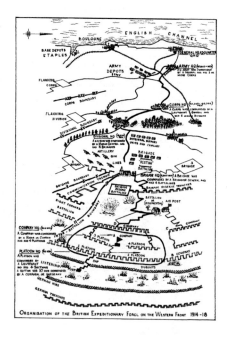

Red Cross nurses behind the lines at the dressing station. (Author's collection)

The Shot at Dawn Memorial was unveiled in 2001, significantly earlier than the posthumous pardons that were granted to the 306 soldiers executed for cowardice, desertion and other offences excluding murder and mutiny. The statue is the work of Andy Decomyn and depicts Private Herbert Burden of the 1st Battalion Northumberland Fusiliers, who was shot on 21 July 1915 at Ypres. He was 17 years of age, although some reports say he was 16 years and 8 months. (Author's collection)

Sub-Lieutenant Edwin Dyett.
(Public Record Office)

A view of Albany Road,
Cardiff, the birthplace of
Sub-Lieutenant Edwin Dyett.
(The Brian Lee Collection)

DEATH WARRANT.

Temporary Sub-Lieutenant E.L.A. DYETT, R.N.V.R. Nelson Bn

having been tried by General Court Martial, and sentenced
to death by shooting, the sentence will be carried out
between 7.30 and 8.30 a.m. at ...*ST. FIRMIN*........
on ..*Friday 5th January 1917.*

C. D. Shute

Commanding 63rd R.N. Division.
....

3/1/17.

Dyett's death warrant. (Public Record Office)

Confirmed ✓

D. Haig. F.M.

2 Jany 17

Confirmed by the Commander-in-Chief. (Public Record Office)

Dyett's grave at Le Crotoy Cemetery. (Author's collection)

A picture of Private William Jones (left) with an unidentified solider friend. (Author's collection)

Private William Jones' name was inscribed on the war memorials nearly ninety years after he was executed. (Author's collection)

Robert King, George Brinley Evans and Tom Marston at the reception following the dedication service of placing Private William Jones' name on the Glynneath War Memorial. (Picture by Glyn Davies)

Plaques from The Shot at Dawn
Memorial in Lichfield, Staffordshire.
(Author's collection)

Private John Thomas
Welsh Regiment
20th May 1916
Aged 44

Private Albert Troughton
Royal Welsh Fusiliers
22nd April 1915
Aged 22

Private George Watkins
Welsh Regiment
15th May 1917
Aged 31

Private Thomas H. B. Rigby
South Wales Borderers
22nd November 1917
Aged 21

Corporal George Povey
Cheshire Regiment
11th February 1915
Aged 23

Private Major Penn
Royal Welsh Fusiliers
22nd April 1915
Aged 21

Private William Jones
Royal Welsh Fusiliers
25th October 1917
Age unknown

Private James Grist Carr
2 Welch Regiment
7th February 1916
Age 19

Chapter Seven

Granting Posthumous Pardons to the 306 Executed Soldiers

Extracts from the House of Commons Debate in 2006 on granting posthumous pardons to the 306 executed soldiers

Dr Lewis: The problem that I have intellectually with what the minister proposes is that he is going to let the convictions stand, and pardon people purely because they were executed. That explains why the 2,700 who were not executed are not being pardoned, whereas the 300 who were executed are being pardoned. I am not sure how that will remove the stigma. Surely the stigma results from conviction rather than execution. If I were a member of one of the families concerned who thought that my ancestor had been wrongly convicted because, for example, he had had shell shock, it would not encourage me to know that his conviction stood and he was being pardoned only because of the severity of the sentence, not because of the injustice of the conviction.

Mr Derek Twigg: I understood the point that the hon. Member for Westbury (Dr Murrison) made earlier about that issue, but anyone who talked to the families and those who have been campaigning would see how important the decision is to removing the stigma and dishonour associated with execution.

The government do not see this as an attempt to rewrite history by quashing convictions or sentences. The pardon does not do that. Our amendment avoids the difficulties that would arise from assessing each individual case under the prerogative. As I have said, its aim is to lift the stigma that has been associated with the executions for far too long, and has affected the soldiers' families most deeply.

Mrs Claire Curtis-Thomas (Crosby) (Lab): The matter is of grave concern to a number of my constituents who had a relative who was summarily killed. They greet this day with great relief, and fully support what my hon. friend is saying.

Mr Derek Twigg: My hon. friend has made an important point. I know how much work she has put into her campaign on behalf of her constituents.

The pardon covers all servicemen executed for offences such as desertion and cowardice committed between 4 August 1914 and 11 November 1918. Regrettably, we have not been able to list individually the names of those receiving the pardon, as our surviving records are not sufficiently comprehensive.

Mr Bob Spink (Castle Point) (Con): The minister is a very generous gentleman. He opened a war memorial in my constituency a week or so ago. Both my father and my grandfather fought, one in the Great War and the other in the Second World War, and they both suffered. I know for certain that if they were alive they would be delighted with what the government are doing, and would want to pass on their thanks and congratulations to the hon. Member for Thurrock (Andrew Mackinlay), the fulfillment of whose campaign we are seeing today. The House should honour him as well.

Mr Derek Twigg: The hon. gentleman reflects a common view, not least among many ex-servicemen and veterans. It was a great pleasure to visit his constituency recently to support the opening of the war memorial. I know of the tremendous work that he did to establish the memorial, along with the local community, and it was an excellent day.

Mr Henry Bellingham (North-West Norfolk) (Con): The key to this decision has obviously been the shell shock that was beyond the control of those soldiers. Is the minister aware that of the 346 who were shot at dawn, five were shot for disobedience of a lawful order, including a member of the Royal Anglian Regiment who disobeyed four separate lawful orders on four separate occasions? In fact, he deserted before he even faced a bullet. For disciplinary reasons and, I believe, quite rightly, he was sentenced to death. Why should those people be pardoned as well?

Mr Derek Twigg: As I have said, there is an issue relating to conviction for wrongdoing and, obviously, disciplinary procedures, but let me return to what we are proposing in relation to the ultimate sentence, execution, and the removal of dishonour from that sentence.

Subject to the will of Parliament, we will place a formal record of the pardon alongside the relevant court martial files held in the National Archives, where they survive. The record will be visible to anyone viewing those files in the future. I believe that it will play an important part in helping to restore the memory of those service men.

In committee in the other place, my noble friend Lord Drayson explained why the government had announced their decision to seek a statutory pardon during the recess. We made our announcement at the earliest possible opportunity following completion of our policy review, so that we could begin the necessary consultation and drafting of an amendment. I am sure the House will agree that once we had reached a decision, and given the age of some of those campaigning for pardons, it was only right for the government not to delay further on this important matter until another opportunity arose in the legislative timetable. For the same reason, we intend the pardon to take effect as soon as the Bill receives Royal Assent.

The subject of pardons is highly emotive. I know from my postbag that the public feel passionately about it. I also know of the considerable interest that Parliament has taken in the matter, demonstrated by the number of Members who are present today. It is right that I should pay particular tribute to my hon. friend the Member for Thurrock (Andrew Mackinlay), and to all other Members who have campaigned tirelessly for a pardon for First World War soldiers. The family of Private Farr – who have been strongly supported by my hon. friend the Member for Harrow, East (Mr McNulty) – and many others have been part of the campaign for pardons, and I salute the role that they have played in the process.

Mr Kevan Jones (North Durham) (Lab): Will my hon. friend give particular thanks for the work done by John Hipkin? John was one of my constituents when I was a councillor on Newcastle City Council. He worked tirelessly on this issue, and was tenacious not only in his campaign but in gaining publicity for it. I hope that my hon. friend will recognise the work that John has done.

Mr Derek Twigg: Many people have worked tirelessly, but I particularly recognise the work that John Hipkin did.

Lord Mayhew of Twysden spoke in support of the amendment in Committee in the House of Lords. In a particularly poignant contribution, he said:

> It is not necessary to take special account of the extreme youth of so many of these soldiers, nor the fact that many of them had volunteered to serve, sometimes falsifying their age to do so. There is quite enough already to show that the humane and just, as well as the constitutionally sound, course is not to overturn the convictions, not to overturn the sentences, not to impugn the decisions of the Commander-in-Chief, but to effect posthumous pardons for these unhappy men.[18]

Official Report, House of Lords, 12 October 2006; Vol. 685, c.424.

This week we remember those service men and women who sacrificed their lives while serving their country in time of war. The First World War claimed many millions of lives, and I believe it is appropriate for us to take this opportunity to recognise some of the other victims of that war, namely those who were executed. I trust that the House will feel able to support the amendment, and bring closure to all the families who have had to live with the stigma of these executions in the period since the First World War.

Mr Gerald Howarth (Aldershot) (Con): I join the minister in paying tribute to the soldier from the Duke of Lancaster's Regiment who has tragically lost his life in Iraq. I am sure that the minister reflected the views of the entire House in sending our condolences to his family.

No one can approach this subject without being moved by the terrible human tragedy involved in the cold execution of soldiers by their brothers-in-arms in the midst of one of the most epic battles in history. No one has done more than the hon. Member for Thurrock (Andrew Mackinlay) in bringing the issue before the House, as he has done persistently and tenaciously for the past thirteen years. I suspect that in the fullness of time this will come to be known as the Mackinlay amendment.

As Colonel John Hughes-Wilson wrote in the journal of the Royal United Services Institute:

> There can be no one who is not moved by the chilling reality of soldiers, often young men who had volunteered to serve their King and country, being tied to a stake, blindfolded and shot by a firing squad, sometimes by comrades from their own regiment. It is an image that has entered the national consciousness and which tugs at the heart of any decent person.

Having said that, it is our duty as Parliamentarians to look as objectively and sensitively as we can at the facts and to assess whether the action proposed by the government in granting blanket pardons is correct, as that inevitably will have the effect of exonerating those who may well be deserving, but will also include those who, by any judgment, are not so deserving. In particular, I submit that we need to exercise great care in applying today's standards to the conditions and mores of a century ago.

The facts are as stated by the Under-Secretary. As the Secretary of State's predecessor, the current Home Secretary, pointed out to the House on 24 July 1998, between 4 August 1914 and 31 March 1920, approximately 20,000 personnel were convicted of military offences for which the death penalty could have been awarded. That does not include civilian capital offences such as murder. Of those 20,000, something over 3,000 were actually sentenced to death. Approximately 90 per cent of them escaped execution and 306 were actually executed. Each and every one of those is a personal tragedy for the soldiers, their families and their descendants. However, it is just 1.5 per cent of all those charged with a capital offence.

Given that this measure is the brainchild of the Secretary of State, many hon. Members will be surprised that he has decided not to present the arguments for bringing it before the House, but has left it to his hon. friend the Under-Secretary, a brand new minister. Perhaps the Secretary of State would like to explain why he has chosen not to – [Interruption] The House will note that the Secretary of State does not want to answer.

What has struck me as so curious in this case is the speed with which the Secretary of State, who freely acknowledged that he approached his new position with virtually no experience of Her Majesty's armed forces, rushed to a judgment so soon after taking over. Given his lack of experience and the fact that he had to brief himself on the workings of the MOD at a time when we are conducting two major concurrent military operations in Iraq and Afghanistan, how could he find the time to assess an issue that deserves very careful consideration?

The Secretary of State's predecessor had undertaken just such a review in less hectic times. As he said in his statement to the House in 1998:

> The review has been a long and complicated process.

He reported that he had reviewed every aspect of the cases, including the medical evidence and the legal basis for the trials – field general courts martial. In respect of the medical records, he said that there was no implicit or explicit reference to any nervous or other psychological disorders. The review had also confirmed that procedures for the courts martial were correct, given the law as it stood at the time. He concluded:

> However frustrating, the passage of time means that the grounds for a blanket legal pardon on the basis of unsafe conviction just do not exist. We have therefore considered the cases individually.

Many are questioning how the Secretary of State came so swiftly to such a contrary position to that of his predecessor, a noted historian who had considered the issue in great detail.

Mr Kevan Jones: I thought that it was too good to last and that the hon. gentleman might welcome something that the government has put forward. Will he say whether he supports what the government is doing, or will we just have the continued attack on the Secretary of State?

Mr Gerald Howarth: The hon. gentleman, with whom I have had the pleasure of serving on the Defence Committee, knows me well enough to know that he will have to wait, for my speech is designed to be taken as a whole.

Many are questioning how the Secretary of State came to such a contrary conclusion to that of his predecessor. Did he consult his predecessor before making his eye-catching announcement? Shall I give way to the Secretary of State? Has he found evidence that was denied to his predecessor? The right hon. Member for Islwyn (Mr Touhig) said in a debate earlier this year that he had found no new evidence. I can only assume that the Secretary of State has found none either.

Has the Secretary of State obtained compelling new legal advice from the Attorney-General, or from anyone else? Clearly not, according to the noble Lord Drayson, who explained in another place:

It is clearly not a traditional prerogative pardon. Unlike a prerogative pardon this measure does not quash convictions or life sentences .

We are entitled to ask what it does do.

Mr Robathan: I do not want to make a cheap point but, as my hon. friend knows, I am not convinced that this is an entirely wise move. Previous Labour governments will have looked at this. Does my hon. friend think that the total lack of experience of military life in the present Labour government has led to the measure being proposed now, as opposed to twenty, thirty or fifty years ago under other Labour governments?

Mr Gerald Howarth: My hon. friend poses a perfectly legitimate question to which I do not know the answer. The Secretary of State will undoubtedly give his justifications. His junior minister has done so and, in welcoming him belatedly to his post, may I say that he did so extremely well and with great sensitivity? However, one is entitled to ask: if the measure does not quash the conviction or lift the sentence, what does it do?

The Under-Secretary said that the aim was to lift the stigma. Many would argue that the stigma has already been removed as the passage of time and changing values have cast in a new light the tragic deaths of those young men, although, self-evidently, not for a number of the families involved. As my hon. friend the Member for New Forest, East (Dr Lewis) said, what about the stigma attached to those 2,700 who were convicted and sentenced to death, but who in the end had their sentences commuted?

We have to consider whether there is a downside to this move by the government. It is important that we in this House consider these matters carefully and look at the full implications of what has been proposed.

Mr Peter Bottomley: I am interested in my hon. friend's speech. Is the matter not summed up by the Lords amendment, which refers to 'recognition as victims of First World War'?

Does my hon. friend remember previous junior Defence Ministers answering debates in the House who were pretty well mauled by the House as a whole, which was arguing for recognition such as is being proposed this evening?

Mr Howarth: I am acutely aware of the sensitivity of the issue. The right hon. Member for Islwyn said that he hoped we could find a solution. He was not able to do so when he was in the department. Clearly, there is an issue, but we have to consider whether there are downsides to the proposal. Ministers have repeatedly asserted that they are not aiming to rewrite history, but many fear that this will create a precedent and are in no way reassured by the familiar Whitehall mantra that there are 'no plans' to extend the pardon to other campaigns, as Lord Drayson has said.

Is it really beyond belief that others shot for desertion during some other battle will not become the object of a further campaign, or that other nations might not seize upon this precedent to demand apologies for acts of war? How would ministers like to be the subject of future generations' judgment on the management of the Iraq war, including their decisions on preparation, deployment and tactics – judged not by today's standards, but in circumstances and according to values that we cannot yet anticipate?

The decision …

> could create precedents for the future and it cannot but have
> the effect of impugning the judgment of the people who made
> those very difficult decisions at the time. It cannot but have the
> effect of revisiting history, which is very dangerous, and putting
> the gloss and judgments of today on decisions made in condi-
> tions which we cannot in our time and at this distance make
> proper judgments about.

These are not my words; they were the words of Lord Ashdown in another place on 12 October. Undoubtedly, it was an extremely fair point.

Mr George Howarth: Will the hon. gentleman give way?

Mr Gerald Howarth: I give way to my right hon. namesake.

Mr George Howarth: Did not my hon. friend the minister make it clear that he was decoupling the decisions made at the time from the decision today to provide a blanket pardon to those affected? By so doing, he is in no way impugning the judgement of the officers who made those decisions in the difficult circumstances of the time.

Mr Howarth: Indeed. My hon. friend and I were on the Committee and we met people who were on active operations. They recognise the importance of discipline. We do not have the death penalty for military operations today, and that is right and proper and reflects the mores of our times. With this amendment, we are dealing with a different society with different mores. That is why we joined the government in resisting attempts in the other place to water down the penalty for desertion.

It is right and proper that we subject the government's proposals to scrutiny, and that is what we have sought to do. However, as we approach the nation's annual service of remembrance we should, and shall, reflect on the courage and sacrifice of those who have fought and died for these islands, for our wider interests and for the values that we hold dear, and those who continue today to lay their lives on the line for our country. Among those whom we remember will be the victims of harsh judgments made in good faith by good men of their day, often in the heat and smoke of battle.

If the amendment brings consolation to the families of those victims, it is a welcome benefit. However, in the interests of justice and for the proper understanding of history, let this be a one-off – a unique – case.

Mr Don Touhig (Islwyn) (Lab/Co-op): It is indeed timely that in this week before 11 November we debate the amendment granting a pardon to 306 of our soldiers shot at dawn in the First World War. Each year, on 11 November, we stand as a nation in silence, mourning and remembrance for all those who made the ultimate sacrifice while serving our country during that bloody, awful war and the conflicts that followed. The people of these islands are a free people today thanks to our war dead. That is a debt we can never repay. We honour their memory and recognise them for the heroes that they are. They have earned the eternal gratitude of the British people.

However, for others no glory is attached to their memory. They have been banished to the fringes of history, their lives forgotten except, perhaps, by their grieving families. They were branded as cowards and traitors, blindfolded and shot at dawn by their own side. Between 1914 and 1920, some 350 men from the United Kingdom, what is now Ireland and what is now the Commonwealth, were executed for capital offences. Seven were Welsh, the youngest of whom was 19. Of the 350, 306 were executed for the military offences of desertion or attempted desertion, cowardice, disobedience, leaving a post, sleeping at a post, casting away arms or striking a superior officer – all offences listed in the amendment.

My right hon. friend the Home Secretary, when he was Minister of State at the Ministry of Defence, sought a way to pardon the 306 who were shot. As has been mentioned, he concluded that there should not be a pardon for some and not others, and he was right. When he became Secretary of State for Defence in 2005, and I was appointed

Under-Secretary, it fell to me to examine the matter further, not least because of the case brought by the family of Private Harry Farr and the concerns expressed by Members of both Houses. I looked at four possible options and I concluded that the only feasible option was a legislative pardon. Before I left the MOD, and with the full support of my right hon. friend the present Home Secretary, I set in train work to prepare for this legislation.

I pay tribute to my right hon. friend the Secretary of State for Defence, who came into the job in May and immediately set about taking forward that legislative pardon, which is why we have the amendment today. My right hon. friend has acted with courage and determination and he has taken a step that others may have been reluctant to take. I also join the appreciation on both sides of the House for my hon. friend the Member for Thurrock (Andrew Mackinlay), who has been determined and persistent in ensuring that the matter did not go away but came regularly before the House. I also know that my right hon. friend the Member for Torfaen (Mr Murphy), when he was Secretary of State for Northern Ireland, received several representations on the issue and I know that he also welcomes the amendment.

This decision is not an easy one for Parliament to take. I have met ex-servicemen who are totally opposed to the idea of a pardon, feeling that those who were shot at dawn had let down their comrades. Others take a contrary view and, with their vivid and often terrible memories of life in the trenches, believe that it is time to pardon the 306.

Mr Ben Wallace (Lancaster and Wyre) (Con): The hon. gentleman listed several offences for which people would be pardoned. He left out the offence of mutiny and sedition, for which two or three of the soldiers on the list were executed. That offence is not linked to cowardice and the Army Act 1881 makes no mention of shell shock or cowardice. That offence is severely damaging to troops in the field, so is he concerned that those found guilty of it will also be pardoned?

Mr Touhig: That point is covered in the amendment and if the hon. gentleman will permit me, I will refer to it in a broader sense later in my speech.

If the amendment is passed, as I hope it is, it should not be seen as a reflection of the failure of those who presided at and conducted the field courts martial that condemned the 306 to a firing squad. Those who presided were doing the duty required of them. They held the king's commission to prosecute a war. They had to maintain discipline and administer military justice as the law of that time prescribed. In my view, they acted properly and honourably in the discharge of that duty.

Some will say that the amendment will rewrite history and judge the actions of 1914 by today's standards. That is a perfectly reasonable argument, although I do not accept it because I do not believe that the amendment condones cowardice, desertion, mutiny or assisting the enemy, as the hon. Member for Lancaster and Wyre (Mr Wallace) suggested a moment ago. Military discipline was and remains the cornerstone of our armed forces' behaviour. However, the amendment is necessary as a recognition of the fact that many – I accept not all – of those shot were suffering from mental illnesses, of which people at the time knew very little.

I have had meetings with the families of some of the men who were shot and I was touched by their quiet determination to see those men pardoned. They were motivated by nothing more than a wish to see their loved ones remembered, without shame, alongside the tens of thousands of others who went to war in September 1914 full of high spirits and pride, but who never came back. I pay tribute to the families' quiet dignity, as many have lived with the terrible stigma associated with having a father, grandfather or great-grandfather going bravely off to war only to be shot by his own side.

The amendment will not ease the pain and heartache that the verdict of the field courts martial caused, but I hope that, in time, it will be seen as having put right a terrible wrong. It is all too easy to forget that the soldiers of the First World War had none of the modern world's benefits of free education and health care. Most of the accused were poorly educated, working-class young men: often, they were inarticulate and illiterate, with no ability to represent themselves in a tense courtroom where life or death was at stake. If all the young men who stood trial were medically examined according to the standards of care enjoyed by our soldiers today, I am sure that the result would not have been that 306 of them were shot.

No one can turn back the clock. The passage of time means that we are left with only the records of the cases, most of which make no reference to the mental or nervous illnesses from which the soldiers were suffering. This week, we will remember our war dead. I hope that, as a country, we can at long last find it in our hearts to pardon and pay our respects to all the young men who lost their lives on the foreign battlefields of the First World War. Whether they were shot by the enemy or by their own side, all were victims of a terrible and bloody war.

Nick Harvey (North Devon) (LD): This is a very delicate matter, and in the debate so far we have heard two different sides of the argument. It has taken us a long time to get where we are today, and I want to join those who have paid tribute to the hon. Member for Thurrock (Andrew Mackinlay) for the persistence with which he has campaigned on this issue.

The two sides of the argument are clear. Some look at the events leading to the executions and call into question how matters were handled at the time. Indeed, many people call into question the conduct of many aspects of the First World War.

In contrast, we have heard that others believe that meddling in these matters is an attempt to rewrite history.

I believe that the government have wrestled with the balance of the argument and that they have come to the right conclusion. The logic of the convictions was articulated by the hon. Member for New Forest, East (Dr Lewis), and one can see how lifting them would bring more comfort and satisfaction, but that really would be an attempt to rewrite history. The same is true of lifting the sentence: although I abhor the capital sentences that were handed down, they were the sentences that applied to such offences at the time. We cannot go back over history and lift the sentences or query the convictions. We cannot remove the pain that followed for those who lost family members in that way – a pain that the descendants have continued to endure in the decades since.

What we can do is to acknowledge and recognise history, with the benefit of the greater knowledge and understanding that we now have of post-traumatic stress disorder. Almost a century later, we as a nation cannot rewrite history or undo the pain, but our modern comprehension means that we can understand, forgive and pardon. The government deserve credit for getting the delicate balance in this matter right. The Secretary of State deserves credit for making a relatively rapid decision in this matter. I do not condemn or criticise him for that, as he has showed a willingness to make other decisions rapidly – notably in procurement, and I think that he deserves commendation for that as well.

The government have come to the right conclusion in this difficult matter. However, I echo the hope that it will not form a general precedent and that the circumstances will be recognised as unique.

Andrew Mackinlay (Thurrock) (Lab): I have been in Parliament for fourteen years, and this evening's debate will probably turn out not to be the most important of my political career. However, supporting this amendment is certainly my proudest moment in the House of Commons. I hope that the House will forgive me if I explain why, as that will buttress the case for the amendment.

First, though, let me say that my hon. friend the Under-Secretary of State for Defence framed and introduced the amendment in a moving and sensitive way. In addition, I very much welcome the initiative of my right hon. friend the Secretary of State, whom I congratulate without reservation. As we have heard, the measure will grant pardons to soldiers executed in World War One after being charged with crimes such as cowardice, desertion, sleeping at their posts, throwing away arms and hitting a superior officer.

For me, this is a very important personal occasion, and my arguments have both spiritual and temporal elements. Spiritually, I was reminded as I prepared for the debate of the words of Psalm 130:

> Out of the depths I have cried to thee, O lord. Lord hear my voice: let thine ears be attentive to the voice of my supplication.

I believe that there has been a cry from heaven for this wrong to be remedied, and that is what this House of Commons will do this evening, on behalf of the nation.

On the more practical side, I must tell the House that soon after I was first elected I went to Tynecot Cemetery to look for the grave of one of the soldiers executed in World War One. At that stage, very little had been written about what happened, apart from one very good book by his honour Judge Anthony Babington, and the great work entitled *Shot at Dawn* by Julian Putkowski and Julian Sykes, which details all the executions.

I wanted to place on record my recognition of what my studies of those executions had taught me, and I put down an early-day motion calling for the men to be pardoned. To my astonishment and surprise, hon. Members right across the House displayed enormous and immediate support in wanting to add their names to the motion, and extensive interest was aroused around the country.

I understand that some hon. Members may be hesitant about pardoning those who were executed, so I hope that I can offer them some reassurance. Although some people oppose the pardons, the measure is overwhelmingly popular around the country. That does not necessarily make it correct, but that popularity has been shown in the support that has been evident in all parties and in consecutive Parliaments. It has also been evident in support for the Bill proposing the pardons that I have introduced six or seven times while I have been in the House. I welcome the initiative of the Secretary of State and the Under-Secretary; we need this measure now.

I want to reply to Conservative Members. They are entitled to a response to their arguments. The Bill that I introduced six or seven times did not include mutiny.

I welcome the amendment because time is now short. I want to deal with the question of whether the measure at this time is still appropriate. I believe that it is, but it will not be for ever. I regret that a Conservative Member shouted out earlier, 'What about Agincourt?' As he did so, I will respond to that point. Agincourt demonstrably is history. The First World War is still a live and relevant issue for us, because each and every one of us have known and loved veterans of World War One. Some are still alive today. The immediate dependants of the executed men are still alive today. The issue cannot be dismissed in the way that people might dismiss the American Civil War or Agincourt. Referring to Agincourt was a poor shot, and I regret that people have said it.

The issue is still very relevant. Judging by my postbag and, I suspect, the postbags of other hon. Members, people still see it as relevant. Their letters may refer to their dad, who never spoke about World War One, but towards the end of his life did so and said that he was on a firing squad or saw people suffering from shell shock. That supports the view that pardons should be granted.

Mr Gerald Howarth: The hon. gentleman has campaigned vigorously on this issue; he makes a special case for these World War One people. Does he regard this case as a one-off, or does he feel that there are other cases? Has he been approached by others? What would be his reaction to other cases?

Andrew Mackinlay: I believe that it is a one-off. It is such an outstanding matter and injustice is so grave. We have the opportunity to heal by accepting the amendment. I have shared with the House the fact that this is a proud occasion for me. If I have achieved nothing else in the House of Commons, I shall be proud if the amendment is accepted tonight and receives Royal Assent tomorrow. I see it as a one-off.

In the Bill that I proposed to the House on seven occasions, I included the options of a blanket pardon or a tribunal of Commonwealth judges to look at each case. I mention that tonight because I am confident that a tribunal would have concluded the same for each case. I say this in response to the legitimate point raised by Conservative Members. People say, 'You are surely not suggesting that all these were good men.' I believe that a tribunal would have concluded that all the trials were flawed, according not to the rules of today but to the rules that applied then. The rules of natural justice have not just been invented. The rules of natural justice required then, as now, that a person should be able to prepare a defence, call witnesses and be properly represented. Every trial was flawed on those counts. Furthermore, no one was given the opportunity of appealing against their sentence. In none of the trials were the rules of natural justice applied.

The point was also made that 2,700 people were sentenced to death but only a few were executed. I believe that that demonstrates how fickle was the decision to execute. There was no rhyme or reason to it. It was like a raffle whether or not someone was executed, which then goes to the heart of the principle of justice. Justice has to be consistent and clearly understood. Those who were executed were simply unfortunate in the draw.

Reference has been made to the Harry Farr case. It has been my privilege to know the widow and daughter of Harry Farr. A gallant lady well into her nineties, Gertie Harris pursued her father's case with the utmost vigour. Certainly the indications are that, had the case come to court, the Ministry of Defence would have lost.

Mr Robathan: Did I hear the hon. Gentleman say that he knew the widow of Harry Farr? Surely she would be about 110 by now.

Andrew Mackinlay: I was privileged to know the widow of Harry Farr. In 1993 I spent a whole afternoon with her. As the hon. gentleman asks, I will tell him. That wonderful old lady, very frail, in her ninety-ninth year, had every one of her faculties. She spoke with great pride that for the first time in so long someone was standing up for her Harry. Everyone now recognises that Harry Farr was shell shocked and should never have been executed in October 1916. She and her daughter Gertie suffered penury as a result of that execution. She told me how she bore that great stigma for so long. So I did know her, and I know what I am talking about. I have given some study to this matter.

Dr Murrison: Will the hon. gentleman give way?

Andrew Mackinlay: I will give way. I will knock this one down as well.

Dr Murrison: I do not intend to attack the hon. gentleman or the case that he is trying to pursue. He has mentioned the daughter and widow of Private Farr, so I presume that he will be disappointed by subsection (4)(b) of the clause that amendment No. 51 would insert, which removes 'any right, entitlement or liability' and therefore confines the measure to gesture politics. It has no substance.

Andrew Mackinlay: It is certainly not gesture politics to the late Gertie Farr or her daughter. They have made it clear time and time again that they want no remuneration or compensation. All that they want is to have the record put straight. That is the view of all the families involved.

Mr Wallace: We have dealt with subsection (4)(b). The widow and daughter of Harry Farr will still be related to a convicted coward. The pardon would not remove that conviction. Is that not a blight on their family?

Andrew Mackinlay: That is not my reading of the legislation, and it is not theirs. They welcome the initiative of the Secretary of State. In any event, I remind the House that I would not start from here. We would have addressed the matter fourteen years ago when I first introduced my early-day motion and my Bill. We would have looked at the cases in greater detail.

During World War One, attempts were made by people like myself in Parliament to raise these executions. They were slapped down and suppressed. There was no candour or debate. The argument was advanced – it had some legitimacy – that the country was in the middle of a conflict. Come the 1920s, the matter was raised by several hon. Members, one of whom was Ernest Thurtle, the Member for Shoreditch. He was slapped down and told that he was wrong.

The point that cannot be escaped is that for seventy-five years it suited the British establishment to suppress the documentation relating to these cases. Now that the documents have become available to families, jurors, politicians and journalists and we see how flawed the trials were, people say, 'It is too late; it is a matter of history.' How very convenient.

Mr Kevan Jones: Does my hon. friend agree that it is remarkable that the amendment was not opposed in the other place and the Opposition Front-Bench spokesman has given half-hearted support to it tonight, yet numerous Conservative Members are clearly opposed to it? Does he believe that, if they feel so strongly, the Conservatives should have amended the Bill in another place or should vote against it tonight?

Andrew Mackinlay: Reference has been made to another place. It cannot be said loudly enough that, among the people who spoke so cogently and clearly in support was a person known to me as Sir Patrick Mayhew, a former Conservative Attorney-General, Secretary of State for Northern Ireland, soldier and officer. Lord Campbell of Alloway, a veteran of Colditz, also spoke in favour. In my view, public opinion is overwhelmingly with us; in particular, people who have experienced combat and seen and endured stress support the measure.

It is perfectly legitimate for Members to question the wisdom of the provision, but it would be wrong if they continued to do so without calling a Division. I understand why they are probing the matter, but I shall welcome the House's unanimous endorsement of the provision, which looks likely. If there is no Division, the decision will be unanimous and that will be the end of the matter. It would be reprehensible if Members who did not divide the House continued to raise objections after the debate, saying that it was wrong to pardon those people.

Mr Bellingham: I respect and admire the hon. gentleman as a campaigner. He has been absolutely tenacious in this campaign and we all respect that, but if we disagree with some of the detail of the provision we are entitled to probe it, and if the amendment is passed, there will be closure on the issue. During the Boer War, there was the famous case of Breaker Morant, an Australian officer who was shot in extremely controversial circumstances. His family apparently want him to be given a pardon. Does the hon. gentleman agree with that?

Andrew Mackinlay: I am not briefed on Breaker Morant. However, I am pleased that the hon. gentleman raised that case, because I am familiar with the consequences of his execution. After that controversy, eighteen years later, the Australian Government made it a condition that none of their soldiers in units serving in the British Empire forces during World War One would be executed. None was, but nobody suggested that the Australian soldiers fought other than like tigers – despite the fact that they did not have the death penalty hanging over them, they still fought like tigers.

The hon. gentleman also said, generously, fairly and legitimately, that this debate would be the end of the matter. That is all I ask. Members should by all means probe and argue, but I hope that if they do not divide the House they will acknowledge that they have concurred by their silence and approved the measure.

Peter Bottomley: I do not want to take up time in the debate, but many who see more benefits than disbenefits in the proposal will not make speeches but will be wholeheartedly behind what the hon. gentleman has been campaigning for and the government have found a way of achieving.

Andrew Mackinlay: I am grateful to the hon. gentleman. It has been a cross-party campaign. I regret that no Irish

Members are in the Chamber, because the campaign united various sides in Ireland, if only symbolically. Private Crozier from the Shankill and Private Sands from the Falls were both executed in similar circumstances. They were ordinary, poor, inarticulate soldiers, as my hon. friend the minister pointed out. They could not articulate their case and were not represented fairly at their trial. A soldier who was unable to advance when ordered to do so, or who ran away – whether they came from Belfast, Dublin, Glasgow, Edinburgh, Manchester, Birmingham, London or elsewhere – was likely to face a court martial and execution. Many officers suffered shell shock, too, but they were likely to be returned to the love and care of their family in England and the best medical attention available. There was unconscious discrimination in the treatment of shell shock.

The question of history has been raised. One of the consequences of the campaign is not the rewriting of history, but writing a chapter of history that has been suppressed. We spend millions of pounds each year teaching history to schoolchildren and university students, so we need to write it with clarity and precision, including the parts that we find uncomfortable. We are now writing that history. Until 1992, the matter was suppressed. It had been suppressed in Parliament; Ernest Thurtle had been refused access to the papers, which were restricted for seventy-five years. There were only the books by Judge Anthony Babington and Julian Putkowski.

Dr Julian Lewis: I entirely agree that this is a matter not of rewriting history, but of writing history. However, the correct people to write history are historians, not politicians.

Andrew Mackinlay: I would argue that point: some people who call themselves historians make it up as they go along. Some of us have been scratching away at this matter for some time to try to find the truth. That is what Ernest Thurtle did as a Back-Bench Member and it is what I and others have tried, and will continue, to do. We will make the information available for historians. In any event, Anthony Babington – a distinguished judge – and Julian Putkowski and Julian Sykes did their best, despite the fact that the establishment did not want the matter aired.

When the Secretary of State indicated to the right hon. Member for Chingford and Woodford Green (Mr Duncan Smith) that a service would be held when we believed that the last Great War veteran had passed on, it was suggested that the nation would draw a line. That is relevant to our debate. Such matters are still relevant to our age, not only because some veterans are still alive and some of their immediate dependants are very much alive, but because we have known and loved people who served in World War One.

The measure is not ideal – no measure we pass covers all the circumstances – but it is generous and fair. It reflects the will of the nation and I commend it to the House.

Mr Keith Simpson (Mid-Norfolk) (Con): I am grateful to be allowed to address the House on this subject. I declare a number of interests. First, I am both a historian and a politician. About thirty years ago, when I was writing some books on the First World War I was lucky enough to interview several hundred First World War veterans. I followed closely the work of Julian Putkowski; many years ago, he and I sat in the Imperial War Museum scrabbling away together. He continued as a postgraduate researcher for many years and produced a series of books.

Secondly, in 1998 I spoke from the Opposition Front Bench in response to the then Minister of State for the armed forces when we held the first parliamentary debate. After looking at the cases of the First World War soldiers who had been executed, he decided that all he could do was to issue a statement of regret. Finally, in January, I introduced a short debate in Westminster Hall on the subject, to which the right hon. Member for Islwyn (Mr Touhig) replied. Almost every Member in the Chamber is wearing a poppy, and the debate about the executed soldiers has much to do with our national consciousness of the First World War – our guilt and our emotions. That war produced one of the highest numbers of casualties suffered by the British Army and the imperial armies. Our European neighbours had of course been only too conscious of such casualties; we had been fortunate enough never to have suffered to such a degree before.

From a British perspective, the First World War has somehow been seen as not such a good war as the Second World War, which was demonstrably between good and evil. The public's interpretation of the First World War does not stem only from folk memories of their fathers and grandfathers. In many ways, the hon. Member for Thurrock (Andrew Mackinlay) is correct; it is history, but near history rather than far. Both my grandfathers served in the First World War. Both were wounded, but they survived.

Certainly, thirty years ago, it was possible to speak to many such veterans. As much as anything else, it all comes down to the fact that the First World War is seen through the prism of the film *Oh! What a Lovely War*, and of *Blackadder Goes Forth*, which features the caricature figures of General Melchett, Baldrick and others. In its last, most evocative scene, the whole cast, except General Melchett, go out into no man's land, and the scene is then freeze-framed. There is a powerful emotional element to the subject.

It always struck me, when I talked to the highly professional members of the army historical branch – I give them great credit for the work that they have done over many years – that the problem is that the record is incomplete, as ministers know.

As the hon. Member for Thurrock says, access to the files was limited for most people, so it is inevitable that there were conspiracy theories about that. The record is incomplete not because it has been weeded, but because of the nature of the war and the nature of some of the field courts martial. Some of the files on individual cases are quite thick, running to twenty, thirty or forty sheets of paper. On Private Farr, there are some half a dozen sheets.

I have concluded that it would be incredibly difficult to ensure a judicial review, in which judges consider each case in turn, although I know that the hon. Member for Thurrock and others were keen on that idea. Such a system would, ultimately, be unfair. I suspect that the judges would clear some people, but that in other cases they would say, 'I'm afraid that under the rules that existed at the time, which carried the death penalty, some people probably should have been executed.' However, there would have been a great tranche of cases in the middle, on which they would have said, 'I'm sorry, but there's insufficient evidence; if we could call witnesses, we could decide.' I reluctantly decided that, however logical the suggestion, that was not the way to go about the matter.

I declare an interest: I have always believed, and still do, that the situation should be left as it is. I can understand why we politicians might want to take a view on past events; after all, the Prime Minister, very soon after taking office, issued a statement of regret about the Irish potato famine. To me, as a historian, that seemed a somewhat simplistic interpretation of what happened, but the Prime Minister had every right to do what he did, although I would have thought it best to leave the matter alone. I have sympathy for the families, and particularly for people who remember what went on, but although we have spent so much time and emotion on the subject – the hon. Member for Thurrock might say, 'And so we should' – we tend to forget, marginalise or take for granted the actions of hundreds of thousands of men. Most of those who fought in the First World War were civilians, and not all of them were young – many were in their thirties and forties; after all, incredibly, the overwhelming majority of soldiers who served in the First World War were volunteers. However, I shall not go down a discursive route and discuss the history of the amazing 'pals' battalions, made up of volunteers.

A significant proportion of soldiers were pre-war regulars, but after 1917 large numbers were, of course, conscripts, so not all soldiers were fresh-faced youths. We should remember that most of them, at different periods in their service, were terrified. When I have talked to veterans of the First and Second World Wars and of Iraq, and to soldiers in Afghanistan, I have found that they were motivated by many things. Because they are British, they are embarrassed to say that they are fighting for Queen and country, but they will frequently talk about their regiment. Usually, however – and there are hon. Members present who have experience of this – they were motivated by small-group loyalty, which basically comes down to a soldier's sense of being part of a team. Soldiers rarely work as individuals; they are a team, and that is how they survive. They survive because they are part of a team in a mortar section, running a heavy machine gun, or in an armoured fighting vehicle. In normal, civilian life, those team members might not get on well together, but as soldiers they work, live and die together, and if one of them decides to leg it, not only do they let the others down, but somebody else has to take over their duties.

When I interviewed veterans of the First World War, I found that many were disgusted and horrified that soldiers had been executed by the authorities, but among others, I found a quiet anger that the well-known company shirker always managed to skive off at a difficult moment, which meant that somebody had to take his place on patrol and put their life at risk. That is a very fine balance, and I can only make the following plea:

we have spent a great deal of time – obviously, public opinion
is that it is important that we should – bearing in mind what
happened to the men who were executed. Some of them did
not deserve to be executed, some were traditional regimental
bad hats, and some were frequent offenders; all were judged
and executed under a law in operation at the time. We should
also bear in mind the great mass of men who were frightened
and frequently tempted to run away, but who, for many
reasons, did not do so.

I remember editing a book twenty-odd years ago called
The War the Infantry Knew, which was largely written by a man
called Captain J.C. Dunn. He was not a regular soldier; he
had served in the yeomanry in the First World War, and won
the Distinguished Conduct Medal, then went back to being
a doctor. He volunteered in 1915, when he was in his forties,
and served for nearly two years with the 2nd Battalion the
Royal Welch Fusiliers. He won the Distinguished Service
Order and the military cross and bar. His DSO was the result
of a failed Victoria Cross application, and he had had both
Siegfried Sassoon and Robert Graves as patients. His diaries
document his eventual breakdown; he later found that he
could no longer trust himself not to duck when a shell came
overhead. His main worry and concern was about showing
fear in front of others. He recognised that the way to deal with
what they call shell shock was to try to rest soldiers as much
as possible. He had a hard-nosed view of desertion. He was
one of only two regimental medical officers to give evidence
to what was called the shell shock committee. The written evidence that he produced, which is in the Royal Welch Fusiliers
museum, is the only evidence submitted to that committee that
is still extant, as the evidence was weeded at some stage.

I was fascinated by the fact that that man, who was in many
ways very sensitive, and who was greatly admired by Robert
Graves and Siegfried Sassoon, firmly believed that the execution

of men convicted of desertion was necessary, not only '*pour encourager les autres*', but because those people had let down their friends, and that was the most important element.

The only option other than leaving well alone or judicial review is a blanket pardon. I do not agree with taking that course, but I understand why the minister has done so. I use my words carefully: it is a political decision – I do not mean a party political decision – such as that made by the New Zealand and Canadian Governments. I have no intention of voting against the Lords amendment, as it represents the will of the other place, but I must say that I do not think that it will bring closure, other than in a parliamentary sense. Debate on the subject will continue. On Remembrance Sunday, at least, we should all remember not only those men who were killed, but those who, like our grandfathers, survived, and did things that most of us would find incredibly difficult to endure.

Mr Mike Hall (Weaver Vale) (Lab): May I begin by adding my condolences to those sent by other Right hon. and hon. Members to the family of the soldier from the 2nd Battalion of the Duke of Lancaster's Regiment who was killed in Iraq today? I wish to put on the record my personal thanks to my hon. friend the Member for Thurrock (Andrew Mackinlay). Several years ago, I was returning from France when I bumped into him. He had just been on a tour of the battle sites, and he told me about his campaign for men shot at dawn in the First World War. I am delighted that an amendment has been tabled that brings to fruition the work that he and other parliamentarians have undertaken.

My grandfather, Private PW443 Thomas McBride, served with the 18th Battalion of the Middlesex Regiment in the First World War. On the night of 24 May 1917, together with Sergeants Till, Matthews and Ward, he went into no man's land in front of the Hindenburg line to dig a communication trench to the German front positions. They worked in full moonlight for three and a half hours under heavy machine gun fire from the enemy. Fortunately, no one was injured and those soldiers were awarded the military medal for their gallantry and service. Their commanding officer, Second Lieutenant Cecil Harold Wight, was awarded the military cross for supervising the work, and received a pension of five shillings a week.

Fortunately, no one in the 18th Battalion of the Middlesex Regiment was shot at dawn, so my grandfather did not face the prospect of being called to serve on a firing squad to dispatch summary justice. Of the 306 soldiers shot at dawn in the First World War who are the subject of the Lords amendment, 254 were privates, fifteen were riflemen, five were drivers, one was a gunner, one was a drummer, one a labourer, two were sappers, one was a trooper, four were sergeants, three were lance sergeants, six were corporals, eleven were lance corporals, one was a second lieutenant and one a first lieutenant. All but two of the 306 soldiers shot at dawn were 'other ranks' and non-commissioned officers. The most senior officer shot at dawn was Lieutenant Edwin Leopold Arthur Dyett, who was a volunteer reserve with the Nelson Battalion of the Royal Navy Division. He was the son of May Constance and W. H. R. Dyett of Rock Ferry; his father, too, was a Royal Navy reserve.

Lieutenant Dyett was executed on 5 January 1917 at the age of 21, and he was buried in the Le Crotoy Communal Cemetery. In many cases, as has been said, the soldiers who were shot at dawn were suffering from shell shock. I was interested to hear about the shell shock committee in the speech by the hon. Member for Mid-Norfolk (Mr Simpson). In a war diary by a member of the 18th Battalion of the Middlesex Regiment, the first mention of the condition appears in June 1916, when it is recorded that men were suffering from shell shock – the diary does not elaborate further. Officers who suffered from shell shock were deemed to be not fit for duty, and were returned home, but that was not the case for other ranks. That is an important point.

We are not close to understanding the full effects of shell shock, but soldiers who suffered from it were subjected to summary justice. They were not properly represented and they were not given leave to appeal. The morning after their court martial, they were bound, blindfolded and had a marker placed over their heart. They were tied to a stake and shot by twelve members of a firing squad, usually from their own battalion. One soldier was given a blank to fire, so that no one could be sure that they had fired the fatal shot.

Remarkably, the families and loved ones of the soldiers who were shot at dawn were told their sons had died as war heroes. Their bodies were buried in Commonwealth War Grave Commission cemeteries across northern France and Belgium where their names are recorded, and they are rightly 'Remembered with Honour'. It is fitting, therefore, that the House should do the right thing and remove the stain on their character.

The full truth of the executions in the First World War has taken an awfully long time to emerge. My hon. friend the Member for Thurrock presented me with a copy of *Shootings at Dawn: The Army Death Penalty at Work* by Ernest Thurtle, who was MP for Shoreditch. The book was published in the 1920s, and the cases it highlights still make for difficult reading. Responding to an intervention, my hon. friend pointed out that the Australian army did not impose the death penalty for battlefield offences. Anyone who has read Field Marshal Haig's diaries will know that he viewed that as a serious weakness that made it difficult to maintain discipline in the Australian army. However, the lack of a death penalty did not stop the Australians from playing a full part in the eventual allied victory in the First World War.

I wish to turn to the case of Lance Corporal 13857 James Holland of the 10th Battalion of the Cheshire Regiment, which was part of the 7th Brigade of the 25th Division of the

3rd British Army. Lance Corporal Holland was shot at dawn. On the night of 19 and 20 May 1916, the Germans launched a heavy bombardment against the British positions at Berthonval facing Vimy ridge. At 5 a.m. on 21 May, the bombardment intensified. At 3 p.m., following a pause, the British front line was once again pummelled by intense enemy shelling, mortar shelling and tear gas. The 10th Battalion of the Cheshire Regiment was stationed at the front line at Berthonval. In a 4-hour period, eighty German artillery batteries positioned along a 1,800m front launched 70,000 shells at the British positions around Berthonval in front of Vimy ridge. That was the heaviest enemy shelling of the war so far. The British trenches were levelled and all communications were severed. The British artillery replied, but to no effect.

At 7.45 p.m., the Germans blew a mine under the British position, lifted their artillery barrage and directed it at the British support lines. At the same time, the German infantry launched a ground attack across the smashed British defences, and crossed our front line, where they met little resistance. The German infantry secured their objectives. The 10th Battalion of the Cheshire Regiment was tasked with holding the flank of the British position during the German onslaught. On 23 May 1916, the British counter-offensive to re-establish a defence line failed. The Germans anticipated the counter-attack and launched their own artillery barrage of heavy shells against the British lines. The British infantry ground assault scheduled for 8.25 p.m. was met immediately with German machine gun fire and repulsed before it began.

On 26 May, the British high command decided that the artillery necessary to support a major offensive to regain our former position on Vimy ridge would be better deployed on the Somme so that our forces would be ready for a planned summer offensive against the Germans. The Germans began to dig in and fortify their positions. The British Army lost 2,500 men between 21 and 24 May 1916. The 7th Brigade of the 25th Division lost 637 men. At some time during the German artillery bombardment – the heaviest of the war so far – followed by a German infantry attack, Lance Corporal James Holland left his post. He was found guilty of cowardice by a court martial, and he was shot at dawn on 30 May 1916. He was the son of Mary and Samuel Holland, who lived at 16 Flower Street at Northwich in my constituency.

Lance Corporal Holland is buried in the Ecoivres military cemetery in Pas de Calais. When my right hon. friend the Secretary of State announced the Government's decision to grant the pardon, his announcement was covered by the *Northwich Guardian*. It interviewed an army veteran from Weaverham in my constituency. Eighty-eight-year-old Harry Littler of Walnut avenue, who served with the British armed forces for six years in the Second World War, said:

> It's worried me all my life. Anyone who has been on a battle-field would know.
>
> Sometimes those chaps didn't know where they were, never mind what they were doing. The sight of some of those poor wretches – some of whom had given their all – their nerves shot to pieces, having to face death by firing squad because of a decision by unknown 'red tabs' and branded cowards, in my opinion was an infamy.

The government has absolute support for what they intend to achieve in the Lords amendment.

At 3 o'clock on Sunday afternoon, the Under-Secretary of State for Defence, my hon. friend the Member for Halton (Derek Twigg) and I will stand at the war memorial at Runcorn. We will do so in the full knowledge that we can pay tribute to those who have fallen in service of their country, giving their today for our tomorrow, as Parliament will have done the right thing and honoured those who were shot at dawn. I therefore urge the House to support the Lords amendment.

Mr Wallace: As a Lancashire MP, I join in the tribute paid to the soldier of the 2nd Battalion of the Duke of Lancaster Regiment who was killed in Basra on Monday. He will have been doing his best for, and with, his comrades, and carrying out the task that the government sent him there to perform. We shall not forget him on Sunday, and I hope that his family derive some comfort from the personal support that I know that the Secretary of State gives to all the victims of the current Iraq and Afghanistan conflict.

I thank the three ministers from the Department for staying for the debate. We do not often see the full complement, on either the Opposition or Government Front Benches. The Secretary of State and the Minister of State for the Armed Forces should be congratulated on staying, and I welcome that they have done so.

War is tragic. It is full of fear, and full of people who do not know what the next day will mean for them. War is confusing, and it separates people from those whom they love, and, very often, young men of all classes and all educations find themselves in positions that they would rather not be in. However, few of them feel that there are people to blame for the position that they are in. They do what they do because they feel that it is the right thing to do at the time. Many of them look back and ask, 'Should I have been doing that? Should I have been in Northern Ireland? Should I have been carrying out the wishes of the government of the day?' However, tragedy – feelings of loss and suffering – is part of war, and that tragedy cannot be picked apart because that suits us by our values of today.

The case that has been put forward for the pardons is, in my view, misguided. Much of that case is also full of inaccuracies. For example, the fact is that we did recognise shell shock at that time, but what we did not do was treat it correctly. We often took officers out of the field and sent them far back to Blighty, where they received what we now know to have been the wrong treatment. Although we got our medical treatment wrong at the time, should we judge the people of the day because their knowledge of medicine was not as good as ours is now?

That case is also full of inaccuracies because the names of many of the people for whom pardons are sought have changed – they have fluctuated. It is interesting that the government cannot produce a definitive list of those who were executed in the war who deserve a pardon. As we know, there is a lack of records. Members of various parties have made it clear that in the cold light of day, perhaps by judicial committee, they could not make decisions on whether a pardon would have been an appropriate way of dealing with some of the problems.

I am mystified that people convicted of 'mutiny and sedition' under section 7 of the Army Act 1881 will be pardoned. Mutiny is not cowardice. Mutiny is not desertion. Mutiny is undermining the very core of military discipline, sometimes for subversive reasons. As many of the French corps and British units in the First World War knew, it can cause catastrophic problems for fighting on the front, and, in the end, it can lead to a breakdown of the whole war effort. I am amazed that a pardon for that has been added.

It is important that we recognise that these are real offences that have a real impact on war-fighting. In today's world, if a warehouse security guard falls asleep, someone comes in and nicks all the stock. But if someone falls asleep on sentry, they might well condemn their men to death – not only in their platoon, but perhaps, in their company. There are plenty of historical war stories of such events occurring in every conflict; they have occurred in Northern Ireland, and they have happened since time immemorial. This is not the kind of issue that we can just move aside because that suits us. Some of these offences have real consequences for other people who were doing their job: hundreds of thousands of such people have died in the First World War and many other conflicts.

It is dishonourable for us in this House, in this century, with our values, to decide whether people of that era would have a different view. I was not around in 1918 or 1916. I know that, as a soldier, I would never have the audacity to compare my military experience today with that of those who were in the military nearly 100 years ago. We all face different challenges in different conflicts, and our values will always be different. For us to go back into the First World War and pick and choose what suits us is an insult to all who fought in that campaign, and all who did their best to make sure that Britain was victorious in a war that would have affected our freedoms if we had failed in it.

The class issue has already appeared in today's debate. There is a romantic notion that General Melchett was condemning people to death from behind the lines. Many of the men concerned were tried by their peers from their battalions, who themselves had been through the same conflicts. People did not appear from nowhere dressed in nice pressed shirts to judge these men; they were often tried by their peers. We might not like the trial process that they faced, but sometimes they faced those trials because of the conditions that people were in – because they did not have the luxury of being able to leave the front line, as they had to get on with doing their job, which was playing their part in defending Britain and ensuring victory in the First World War. We should not be persuaded by such romantic visions, or by the comedians whom we often see on television.

Mr Kevan Jones: Does the hon. gentleman not agree with me that, as was said by the hon. Member for Mid-Norfolk (Mr Simpson) in his eloquent speech, officers who were exposed to shell shock were sent home, whereas privates from working-class communities such as mine were sent before the firing squad?

Mr Wallace: The hon. gentleman misses the point. They were sent home by people in that era, making judgments on their values, not our values. I do not think that that is the right way to go about such matters, but that was the way they went about it, and who am I to stand here and judge them? Such decisions were based on a class system that is, I hope, on its way to being defunct, but that system was historical fact, even if it is not of today. Therefore what the hon. gentleman says is not the right argument to use as an excuse for pardons.

Mr Jones: I take on board the hon. gentleman's point, but that stain is still on the character of those families in working-class communities throughout this country; it has not been erased through the passing of the generations. That might not affect the middle-class homes that the hon. gentleman might want to represent in this House, but for working-class communities, that stain is there, and it has been there for generations.

Mr Wallace: That is the most patronising pap that I have heard for a long time.

Mr Keith Simpson: Can I intervene on what sounds a little like an old-fashioned class-war disagreement? I do not think that we should go down that route. I, as a military historian, accept that, at that time, an officer's chances of being executed were far less. However, I also must say that the soldiers convicted and executed during the First World War of a capital punishment came from wide and varied backgrounds. They were not all inarticulate working class by any means. I think that we should now continue by listening to the main line of the eloquent speech of my hon. friend the Member for Lancaster and Wyre (Mr Wallace), rather than get drawn down this negative route.

Mr Wallace: I am grateful to my hon. friend for his advice. I certainly agree that this debate is not about class, and that it is not about today's values. A lot of it is about yesterday's historical values.

Patrick Mercer (Newark) (Con): Does my hon. friend agree that the hon. Member for North Durham (Mr Jones) has not quite put his finger on the point, and that he should look with a little more historical accuracy at the sort of men who, certainly by late 1915, were being commissioned and were taking the brunt of the infantry platoon commander's battle? Many of them came from working-class backgrounds, as he might define them.

Mr Wallace: I am grateful to my hon. friend for that clarification. We must recognise that the stigma will still be there. The amendment states that the relevant section that gives a pardon to those who were executed does not 'affect any conviction of sentence'.

I take that to mean that there will still be people convicted of cowardice, desertion and all the other offences, and that is stigma enough. Regardless of whether or not I was executed, I would not like to have a conviction for cowardice.

This is the problem with the amendment and the gesture politics behind it. If the government wanted to grant a pardon, they should have tabled an amendment that granted a proper pardon, rather than one that removes the stigma only for those who were executed, and not for those who were convicted. That is the flaw in the amendment – that stigma will still be there for those war widows and others for generations to come. I would welcome some clarification from the government on this issue. Will such people still have a conviction?

Mr Touhig: The pardon is not perfect, and there are matters – the hon. Member for Mid-Norfolk (Mr Simpson) discussed them – that cannot be covered. There is no perfect solution to this problem, but if the hon. Member for Lancaster and Wyre (Mr Wallace) felt that this was the wrong amendment, it was open to him and his colleagues to move a better one. We all want closure and a resolution to this issue, in the interests of those who suffered and of the families who still suffer.

Mr Wallace: My idea of closure is to learn from history and not tinker with it. We should recognise the tragedy that was the First World War, warts and all. This should not be about tinkering in order to make us feel good in our beds. If we do not learn from history, we will not learn for the future. I hope that this government recognise that we in this House are at our worst when we are pious and apply our values to yesterday, rather than learning the lessons of yesterday and taking them forward, in order to avoid such tragedies and such loss and hurt to our country.

Mr Kevan Jones: I rise to support the amendment, which I believe is the correct way to put right a dreadful wrong done to many people in my constituency, and others. I accept and respect the fact that there is an alternative position. It was a pleasure to listen to the hon. Member for Mid-Norfolk (Mr Simpson), who explained his position in a well informed, thoughtful and well argued speech, but who recognised that there must be some form of closure. I disagree with his conclusions, but I respect his position.

What I cannot accept, however, is what we have heard tonight from Opposition Front Benchers. They have criticised the Secretary of State for taking this decision – I congratulate him, and I also congratulate my right hon. Friend the Member for Islwyn (Mr Touhig) on his part in the amendment – but they have not got the guts to vote against the amendment tonight. It was open to the Opposition to table amendments in another place, but they have not taken that opportunity. That would have been a far more respectable position to adopt.

The hon. Member for Blaby (Mr Robathan) – he is not in his place – sought to imply that, because the three ministers on the Front Bench have not got military experience, they are somehow dabbling in the military process. If the hon. gentleman were here, I would tell him that he should take a look at his own Front Benchers. There is the honourable exception of the hon. Member for New Forest, East (Dr Lewis), who is a naval reservist. I think that the hon. Member for Aldershot (Mr Howarth) made the Air Cadets and no further, and unless –

Mr Gerald Howarth: Just to put the record straight, the hon. gentleman knows perfectly well that I was commissioned in the Royal Air Force volunteer reserve as a member of my university air squadron.

Mr Jones: And did not go any further.

The nearest that the hon. Member for Forest of Dean (Mr Harper) got to action in the trenches – unless he has not told the House about his military record – was defending against the critics in his role as operations manager from 2000 to 2002. So the criticism levelled at ministers for taking this decision, and the argument that they do not understand the military, is completely unworthy of this debate.

Mr Robathan: Will the hon. gentleman give way?

Mr Jones: With pleasure.

Mr Robathan: I am grateful to the hon. gentleman; I had not intended to rejoin this debate. My aim was not to attack the ministers on the Front Bench, for whom I happen to have – to varying degrees – grudging regard, but to point out that when Major Attlee was Prime Minister and when that famous Labour Prime Minister Ramsay MacDonald was in power, they took no action. What has changed except the passage of ninety years? The hon. gentleman has been attacking my hon. friends, but I should point out that we in the shadow government have a very large number of people with military experience, including myself, my hon. friend the Member for Westbury (Dr Murrison), who has been in Iraq, and my hon. friend the Member for North-East Milton Keynes (Mr Lancaster).

Mr Jones: I am well aware of that and I have to pay tribute to people such as the hon. Member for North-East Milton Keynes (Mr Lancaster), who serves on the Defence Select Committee and who has been in Afghanistan over the summer. I am sorry, but I will not accept this nonsense that, because people have not got military experience, they are somehow inferior to those who have served in our armed forces. To say that is not to criticise those Opposition Members – or anyone else in this House – who have served in Her Majesty's armed forces.

I want to pay tribute to my hon. friend the Member for Thurrock (Andrew Mackinlay), who has campaigned tenaciously for this amendment; it is a great tribute to his persistence. I also want to pay tribute to John Hipkin, who was a constituent of mine when I was a city councillor in Newcastle-upon-Tyne, and who has fought for many years for the pardon that the House will hopefully agree to tonight. John, a cabin boy, was the youngest prisoner of war during the Second World War, and as my hon. friend the Member for Thurrock reminded me, he featured in a documentary last year that showed the pressures he experienced serving his country as a teenager.

The amendment will not solve every single problem, and if we are looking for perfection we will not find it there, but it will enable a line to be drawn under these events.

Lance Corporal Peter Goggins, of South Moor, Stanley – he is the uncle of a constituent of mine, Marina Brewis, who also lives in Stanley – was shot at dawn in 1917. He and his comrades, who were part of the 19th Durham Light Infantry, were guarding their positions on the western front. They were retreated when a senior officer informed them that an ambush was taking place that was advancing from the German lines. That proved to be unfounded, and Corporal Goggins was tried on Christmas Eve 1916 and executed in January 1917.

Private Albert Rochester witnessed the execution. His diaries state:

> A motor ambulance arrives carrying the doomed men. Manacled and blindfolded, they are helped out and tied up to the stakes. Over each man's heart is placed an envelope. At the sign of command, the firing parties, 12 for each, align their rifles on the envelopes. The officer in charge holds his stick aloft and, as it falls, 36 bullets usher the souls of three of Kitchener's men to the great unknown.

The military chaplain present said of the three men executed that morning:

> Braver men I have never met.

This amendment will lift the stain on the Brewis family. When Mrs Brewis, who is now 71, heard of the amendment, she said that it was 'wonderful news', and that although she would be 'sceptical' until Parliament passed it, she and the other families who have been campaigning for a pardon for many years would be delighted to see it.

This has not been an easy decision for ministers and others to reach, but it will lift the stigma and the sense of shame that a lot of such families have experienced. We must also remember the hardship that they went through, as my hon. friend the Member for Thurrock explained earlier. I accept that there are Opposition Members who do not agree with the amendment, and if they feel very strongly that they cannot support it, they should divide the House and ensure that we put on the record who supported the amendment and who did not.

Mr Bellingham: As far as that last set of remarks is concerned, many of us have listened to this argument very carefully, and many of us may disagree with parts of the proposal, but we have a right to question the government, to hold them to account and to ask various questions. Just because we do not go along with everything that the Hon Member for North Durham (Mr Jones), has said, that does not mean that we should necessarily push the amendment to a vote. I do not understand the logic of what he has been saying.

I should declare an interest because both my grandfathers fought in the First World War with huge bravery and distinction. My great-uncle also fought in the First World War as a founder member of the Royal Tank Regiment. Umpteen relations of mine fought in the First World War and died. The issue is very emotional.

We have had an interesting debate tonight. I admire the hon. Member for Thurrock (Andrew Mackinlay), whom I have respected for many years. We have campaigned together in other areas and he has been a marvellous ally in one particular campaign involving constituents who have faced injustice. I greatly admire his tenacity and determination. Obviously we should salute that this evening, because he has worked tirelessly on this matter. I do not agree with where he is coming from and I do not support the conclusions that he has reached, but I still respect him for that.

My hon. friend the Member for Mid-Norfolk (Mr Simpson), who is my parliamentary neighbour, made a learned and erudite speech. He knows a huge amount about this subject. He made one point that certainly had resonance, because I remember my grandfather making the same point clear to me when we discussed the issue, which we did many times. My grandfather lived until about 1970. He was badly wounded in 1916. He was then badly gassed the following year and never really recovered. I was quite young – about 12 or so – when he died, but I remember speaking to him at length about this issue. He said that he and his friends fought first for their chums, secondly for their regiment, and thirdly for Queen or King. That was the point that my hon. friend made: there was a feeling among the millions of people who fought in the First World War that those who let the side down put not just their own lives, but the lives of many others, at risk.

Successive Secretaries of State have looked at the issue. It is nothing new. I had the privilege and honour of serving as Parliamentary Private Secretary to my right hon. and learned friend the Member for Kensington and Chelsea (Sir Malcolm Rifkind) – he was then the right hon. and learned Member for Edinburgh Pentlands. We looked at the issue in great detail and decided that it would be wrong to reopen the matter and rewrite history. Successive Labour Secretaries of State have done exactly the same. I well remember the right hon. Member for Airdrie and Shotts (John Reid) making it clear that he felt that this was not the right way to go. He argued persuasively and with huge intellectual rigour that pardons should not be granted. I do not know what has changed.

As my hon. friend the Member for Aldershot (Mr Howarth) pointed out, this is a complicated process that involves a great deal of effort and input. With great respect to Labour and Liberal Democrat Members, and indeed some Conservative Members, it beggars belief that ministers can devote time to this matter – important as they may regard it – when they face so many other priorities and issues. Just look at the huge challenges in Iraq and Afghanistan. There is the huge issue of the vehicles in Afghanistan and Iraq that do not have the necessary armour and the issue of helicopter lift capacity. There are all those other massive challenges that my hon. friend referred to.

I know, because I have a large number of friends in the armed forces, including five colleagues from university who happen to be brigadiers or generals, that this decision is very unpopular with the armed forces. I am concerned that the trust and respect of the armed forces for the Ministers of Her Majesty's Government will be damaged by this issue. I only hope that that will be got over quickly. As a number of my hon. friends have pointed out, the decision is totally illogical. It does not quash convictions and it does not remove sentences.

Mr Mike Hall: Will the hon. gentleman give way?

Mr Bellingham: I want to be brief, because we need to make progress. There is a long list of amendments. I am going to wrap my remarks up quite soon.

What about the 2,700 soldiers who were sentenced to death, but had their sentences commuted? Will they be affected? Will they receive a pardon? We heard about the Farr case, which was moving and tragic. However, every single case is different. If one has a look at the breakdown, as some colleagues have already, one sees that out of the 346 soldiers who were executed, thirty-seven were executed for murder and will not benefit from the pardon. I mentioned earlier in an intervention that there were five who were executed for disobedience to a lawful order. One of them was a private in the Royal Norfolks who disobeyed four separate orders, on four different occasions. He was given umpteen warnings. He was sentenced to death by firing squad for disobedience to those lawful orders before he even got near the front, so he certainly could not have suffered from any form of shell shock. As my hon. friend the Member for Lancaster and Wyre (Mr Wallace) pointed out, eighteen soldiers were sentenced for mutiny and various other offences.

The issue is complicated and every single case is different, which is why I took the view that perhaps we should have set up a tribunal of commonwealth judges or learned judges to look at every single case totally separately on its merits. In my judgement, what we are doing is illogical. Whatever colleagues say, if we're not rewriting history, we are certainly writing it. What happened in the Great War was horrific and tragic, but we are looking at it from a modern-day perspective. We are imposing our modern-day values on events that happened nearly 100 years ago. Of course those men would not have been executed today. In the Second World War, there was not a single British soldier executed by firing squad. I gather that one American was executed during the Battle of the Bulge. To put that into perspective, 10,000 German soldiers were hung [*sic*] for either desertion or cowardice in the last war and 25,000 Russians were shot by firing squad – probably double that number were shot by the commissars who were attached to each single unit. Should we really be questioning the motives and the rationale of the army commanders in World War One? Should we be questioning the decisions taken by the much-reviled Field Marshal Haig? How far back should we go? Should we go back to the Boer War and Breaker Morant, or the Zulu War, or the Crimean War? What other categories of offence will be covered by future initiatives of this kind? What about the British traitors who were hanged during the Second World War, such as Lord Haw-Haw and John Amery and many others, who may well not have had a fair trial at the time?

We have had an interesting and, in many ways, moving debate, with a lot of excellent contributions. Those of us who have doubts about this matter should not be taunted by the other side for not putting it to a vote, because we have asked a lot of sensible questions. Can the minister really give us a categorical assurance that this measure will not set a precedent? Is this really a one-off? We are all decent, compassionate human beings. Of course we can regret the past and observe the deeds of our ancestors with astonishment, incomprehension and even sad regret. Obviously we can feel only pity towards those luckless soldiers who were executed nearly a century ago. There is little doubt that many of them showed incredible bravery and astonishing mental toughness when they were finally led out to be shot, blindfolded and alone. We have to applaud their courage in extremis. They were as much victims of that war as the three quarters of a million of their comrades, in addition to the millions of other soldiers, who were killed. However, I do not believe that we should reinvent the past to suit our wishes today. That way lies madness. That is why I have serious regrets about what the government are doing and I am looking forward to the assurances from the minister.

Derek Twigg: With the leave of the House, Madam Deputy Speaker we have had a reflective, important and well-thought debate. No one could say that the arguments expressed by hon. Members on both sides of the House have not been well aired. Strong views have been expressed by many, and passionate views have been expressed by some. This is a difficult issue.

It is important that I put it on record that the intention of the pardon is to remove the dishonour of execution. It is not intended that it will quash the convictions or sentences. It stands as recognition that execution was not a fate that servicemen deserved. I cannot make any clearer why we wish to introduce the measure.

I know that such matters have a great emotional impact on people. We are of course discussing the period of the First World War, which, as the hon. Member for Mid-Norfolk (Mr Simpson) made clear, has a particular impact on the nation's consciousness, given the terrible horrors that took place. I never met my grandfather because he died well before I was born, but I have met and talked to veterans of the First World War, so I have some understanding, albeit perhaps not in the greatest depth, of their suffering, fear and bravery and the horror of the events. Hundreds of thousands of people made many sacrifices and went through absolutely unbelievable experiences in the trenches and during the battles that took place.

On Remembrance Sunday, we will all remember the tremendous courage and sacrifice of those who fought in the First World War, Second World War and other conflicts, and the service that they gave. I hope that we can now let the matter rest in peace.[19]

* * *

Don Touhig makes reference during the debate that seven Welshmen were executed for the offences that the pardons cover. This is accurate but nevertheless emphasises the confusion that exists with this subject; one regularly sees different figures mentioned. The general method of calculating the various backgrounds of the men who fought in the Great War is by the regiment that they were attached to. There lies the confusion because men of various nationalities would have been members of Welsh regiments and, likewise, Welshmen belonged to English regiments. And with many of the records destroyed in the Second World War, it can make tracing the actual birth places difficult.

Interestingly Don Touhig, an MP representing a Welsh constituency, makes reference to a Welshman who was shot at dawn being only 19 years of age. He was undoubtedly talking about Private William Jones from Neath, whose age is banded about as being 19, but he was probably younger. The National Memorial Arboretum in Litchfield, Staffordshire makes no reference to his age on the 'shooting posts' that bears his name at the shot at dawn memorial. This suggests he was underage.

Andrew Mackinlay, the Labour MP, has for many years been one of the most persistent advocates in the quest to gain pardons for those unfortunate soldiers. In the important debate referenced above, his passion is clear in the language he uses to promote his argument. He's been questioned and even ridiculed at every turn, which is illustrated when he's challenged about knowing the widow of Harry Farr. But he's remained steadfast in his resolve and, with the passing of this amendment to the Army Act, his work on the subject sees some sort of justice for those men.

Chapter Eight

The Firing
Party

Following the general or/and court martial that had found
a soldier guilty of one of the offences that carried the death
penalty, the decision and the recommendations of the trial
judges would be sent back to headquarters. There the ultimate
decision would be made – there was no appeal procedure – and
if the paperwork was signed 'confirmed' the process was swift.
There was no obligation on the immediate officer in charge of
the condemned man to inform him before the evening parade.

Whilst on parade the unfortunate soldier would be brought
from his holding room or cell together with his escort, very often
ignorant about what was to follow. The court's final decision and
that of the commander-in-chief was promulgated in front of the
whole battalion. A medic and a padre would be in attendance.

The words 'shot at dawn' would have reverberated through
everyone's mind.

Once the news had been broken to the battalion, the man
was led back to his holding room along with the padre who
would stay with him, helping him to write a last letter home
and/or trying to made his peace with God, until day broke.
He would also be present at the execution.

The selection of a firing party would have held a dread for every soldier in the particular battalion with which the victim served and to any other battalions in the immediate area. No one would have wanted to be selected to make up that number.

On soldier is recorded as saying that after been chosen as a member of the firing party, he had heard that it was the one order a soldier could refuse. He went to his superior and declined. He was replaced and no action seems to have been taken against him. But this behaviour was, it seems, the exception more than the rule; a soldier is conditioned to obey the last order given.

Others would have endured a sleepless night if the order had been conveyed that they had been detailed to execute 'one of their own'. And even if the orders to make up the number were withheld until the following morning, those who could be selected would get much sleep.

The death site would have been identified and on the fateful morning the machinery of the procedure was very swift.

In some reports the accused was led out and walked calmly; others say that alcohol or a shot of morphine was given to the condemned; some records from the field, usually in the form of letters or diaries, say that the victim was dragged to the firing post.

The firing party would be marched about 15 to 20 feet in front of the man, who would have had his legs and arms tied and a blindfold wrapped around his eyes. The medical officer would pin a piece of white cloth over the man's heart and the padre would say something from the Bible and then step back.

There would be one rifle holding blanks, the idea being that no one member of the firing party could be sure that he had actually shot the man dead, although anyone who is well practiced in firing guns will know if the round is live or not by the rifle's recoil. So it would have been a futile gesture but one that probably carried some psychological value.

There were no oral signals. The officer would drop his arm as a sign to fire and simultaneously there would a rack of gunfire and the man would be dead. If he was not, and in numerous reports we read of the medical officer declaring that life was not extinct, then the victim would have a revolver placed to his temple by the officer, who would then pull the trigger.

When the medical officer had declared life extinct, the body would be rolled up in a blanket or sheet and placed in a make-shift grave. The body would be buried in a cemetery at a later date, if the makeshift grave could be located in the confusion of war – as in the case of George Povey from Connah's Quay.

The effect on the firing party would have been utterly demoralising. One report from a soldier in a firing party states that the men were so distraught that they were given two weeks' leave and the soldier says in a diary entry: 'We were shattered so they sent us away on leave. What a way to get leave.'

Many of the men would say in later years that the memory of either taking part in the firing party or being made to witness the execution left a mark on them so deep that only their own death could exorcise it.

Some of the condemned refused to have a blindfold, pre-ferring to stare death in the face. That would not have done members of the firing party much good. Other reports speak of the utter bravery of those facing death. This was not the death that millions of infantrymen suffered going over the top – then they had the thought of immortality by being in great numbers – this death was alone and perpetrated by one's fellows.

'This is wonderful,' said one Irishman, 'I volunteered to fight the enemy and now you are shooting me.'

In 2015, The History Press plan to publish a book currently entitled *We March Back to Breakfast* which will provide a more concise record of those who lined up to perform the military execution.

Chapter Nine

The Following
Years

In the years following the Great War, radically minded
Members of Parliament continued to ask questions regarding
the men who had been executed on the Western Front. Those
families who were aware that fathers, sons, brothers, etc. had
been shot started to petition their own MPs regarding the fate
of their relatives. Sadly many families remained unaware of
how they had died: 'died of wounds' hid the actual reason as
opposed to the phrase 'died in action', which implied they had
died honourably.

The names of those executed did not appear in lists of
'soldiers who died in the war' and it was the Imperial Graves
Commission (now called the Commonwealth War Graves
Commission) that requested them in order to carry on with
the work of erecting headstones over the known bodies in the
many, many cemeteries across Northern France and Belgium:
a piece of land that will forever be England, Wales, Scotland,
Ireland, New Zealand and Canada and a mixture of the other
countries within the British Empire. The omission of Australia
is because the Australian Government would not concede to
the British Government that its soldiers should be executed

under the Army Act, despite Douglas Haig arguing that he should be able to exact the ultimate penalty on the volunteer soldiers from that country to enable the army to maintain discipline. This was the Australian Government's standpoint from the beginning of the Great War and in any conflicts thereafter. Although one Australian soldier was executed, he was serving in the New Zealand Army at the time.

From the 1920s onward the subject of military executions was often discussed, particularly the reasons why soldiers would offend, knowing in the majority of cases that they could be executed. The medical condition commonly called shell shock was usually the basis for the debates. In April 1920, Lord Southborough in the House of Lords made the request to the government to hold an inquiry into the various types of hysteria usually called shell shock. He wanted a focus on its effect on soldiers in the Great War and on the death penalty suffered by them having been found guilty of cowardice.

He reasoned that, now there was greater understanding of the condition and how it not only affected those men who were fighting on the front but also in civilian life, and how those shell shocked had a variety of types of hysteria or traumatic neurosis.

Consider that there were more than 3,000 courts martial held during the Great War for cowardice, desertion, etc. and that so much trauma would have been suffered from the effects of guns and sudden explosions very near to the soldiers; that the men experienced terrible conditions, walking past or sometimes on dead soldiers; suffering extreme fatigue. Many would have been ill-suited to fight in the trenches, through physical weakness or a passive nature. Most would not have handled a gun before and would have only received the minimum of training – it is little wonder that they succumbed to a form of mental illness which would have provoked irrational behaviour.

Lord Southborough stated:

> It is a fact that a true identification of the disorder was wanting in
> the early months of the war, then I fear that, through inadvertence
> and want of knowledge, dreadful things may have happened to
> the men who had in fact become irresponsible for their action.[50]

Lord Southborough understood the position that the generals
were in when receiving the findings of the courts martial during
the war: the main driving force was to maintain discipline and an
efficient fighting force. He also made the point that the majority
of the men who had been either regular soldiers, volunteered
or been conscripted had remained, despite the carnage, sound
of mind.

Continuing, Lord Southborough noted:

> One might expect that boys taken from the plough, the factory,
> or office stool would in some cases crack on the sudden exposure
> to the inferno of fire, noise, blood and death to which they were
> exposed. The ever-present and glorious wonder is that the vast
> majority stood firm and sound of mind and body to the end.[51]

He said that any soldier unfortunate enough to suffer from
a mental condition brought on by his experiences in the war
could well suffer a loss of willpower and cease to have control
over his actions. He questioned if the wartime courts in the
field were considering accused soldiers' mental condition when
the offence had been committed.

In supporting Lord Southborough's motion, Lord Horne
said that there could have been occasions where injustice had
led to a man being executed:

> If there was the shadow of doubt, if there was any suspicion
> that the crime committed might have been caused by any

of the forms of hysteria which are included under the term 'shell shock', I may confidently state that the sentence was not confirmed until the accused had been under the observation of medical authorities.[52]

Lord Horne was speaking only a year or so following the war and could well have been led to believe that doctors' or medics' opinion was at the forefront of the evidence presented to courts martial. We know now that this was not the case in many of the trials and one opinion of a medical officer examining a soldier with shell shock is disturbing, as he says the solider being examined is 'worthless, a coward and [he] had no time for his type. I resolved to give him no help at all.' Damning evidence in trial.

Both the House of Commons and the House of Lords considered the Army and Air Force Act in its Annual Review in various motions and committees without achieving a great deal. The Interdepartmental Committee published its report on 1 April 1925 and did propose that some offences committed whilst on active service and punishable by death should be abolished. That recommendation was good on paper but Parliament was unimpressed.

Ernest Thurtle MP, with dogged determination, ploughed on with campaigning to get the death penalty removed from the Army Act. He had been a serving soldier in the Great War, volunteering in 1914, and served in France. He was discharged from the army in 1919 after being severely wounded. Following his discharge he became active in various matters that affected discharged soldiers and was prominent in convincing Winston Churchill that those soldiers who had been imprisoned for offences committed during the war should be released. He opposed conscription and the death penalty imposed for crimes committed by soldiers, but it was the campaign to secure posthumous pardons for those shot at dawn victims that became a focus in his life. He was the son-in-law of George Lansbury MP, a pacifist – but this relationship didn't stop him volunteering to fight in the war.

He entered the House of Commons when he was returned as the Labour Party member for Shoreditch in 1923 and ended his parliamentary career representing Shoreditch and Finsbury. He died in 1954.

Five years after entering the House of Commons, Thurtle saw some progress in his attempts to have the death penalty for military offences abolished. The government in 1928 relented and eight offences punishable by death were abolished. However, both cowardice and desertion were retained.

The Labour Party then won a majority and formed the government in 1929. Thurtle must have felt like a greyhound breaking fast from the traps at the opportunity to have legislation passed in respect of all military crimes. He lobbied hard and was successful in convincing a majority of the members in the House of Commons to remove the death penalty for cowardice and desertion.

The House of Lords stalled the parliamentary process by rejecting the proposal, following lengthy speeches by military members including Lord Allanby. The Conservative objectors to the move in both Houses were scuppered when the Commons went over the Lords' objections and royal assent was granted on 29 April 1930.

Seven years after landing in the House of Commons, Ernest Thurtle had achieved one of his main objectives.

The death penalty for both mutiny and treachery were not included in the abolition of the ultimate sentence and both offences saw executions in the Second World War on four occasions.

An amazing communication sent from the Ministry of Pensions to the War Office is dated 14 August 1939. It regards the notification of the wording to be used when notifying next of kin in a case of a sentence of death and was referring to the anticipated Second World War – despite the legislation being more than nine years old.

It was to take a further seventy-six years for legislation to follow that would pardon those who committed the offences whilst engaging in hostilities on the Western Front and were shot for them. The acceptance of mental illness that would undoubtedly have contributed to the commission of those offences would, at last, be recognised.

For those soldiers who returned home following the conflict, many would have been broken both physically and mentally. The employment conditions would not have changed a great deal and many, if they were medically able, returned to their various occupations. But their experience would have dominated their lives, often leaving them in deep despair. The effect on their families, too, would have been devastating. Mothers, wives, daughters and girlfriends who would have lived, quite literally, from one home leave to the other, welcomed the Armistice and prayed that the dreaded telegram would not arrive in those last days. The euphoria that families would have experienced to see their loved ones walk through the garden gate would have been met with relief and gratitude that would have been overflowing. The behaviour of the men in many cases would have altered: fits of depression, long periods of silence, sometimes violence directed at those closest to them, and the nightmares that would have haunted them in their fitful sleep.

Some resorted to alcohol and were dismissive of any form of deity, alternatively some became devoutly religious. Extreme emotions were displayed in many ways, which added pressure to the living conditions of the home.

The work patterns of the women who had waved their menfolk goodbye as they left for the front reverted to what it had been before the war. Now child bearing and domestic duties prevailed once again.

Many soldiers would become introverted, refusing to talk about what they had seen and done: their opinions were their own and not to be shared. Where there were once cheerful young men with a life before them, they had aged drastically in only a few years. They all carried on whilst holding, harbouring memories. Some were resourceful and talking helped them, others wrote down their feelings and experiences, but they were all changed forever. The various families in the same area who did see their menfolk return had each other. For those who did not, there was only the fading sepia photograph on the mantelpiece and that condoling telegram from the War Office informing them that he had died for his country.

And there were the families of those men who were executed on the front. For those who did know that their nearest and dearest had been shot at dawn, the loss and shame would have been devastating. The pensions that would have been paid to the families of a man who was lost in action would have been withheld; the medal entitlement they would have earned was also not given. All too soon through gossip, the story might have become known in the locality and when that happened some families disappeared from the area where they lived. One family had a very tragic story: the soldier's mother died of a heart attack and his wife committed suicide, leaving her children orphans.

After the war, when war memorials were being organised, the names were omitted despite the Imperial War Graves Commission commemorating the executed men in the same way as those who had died honourably.

Some Great War memorials read 1914–1918, others 1914–1919, the reason being that the treaty declaring peace was not actually signed until the middle of 1919. Fulstow, Lincolnshire, a village in England that lost several men in the war, was incensed when the village committee was told that one name was to be left off – a man who was executed. The villagers there resolved that if *all* the names could not be engraved on the stone obelisk, then none would be. And that is how it was until relatively recently, when all the names were honoured in the centre of their village.

Some villages and towns in Wales are yet to see the names of those executed placed on the memorials. Hopefully this will be done, but it takes people to believe that the successful campaign to grant posthumous pardons was the right thing to do. Otherwise those names omitted will continue to drift in anonymity, their memories forgotten. In some cases the families are no longer in the area, so it is possible that any distant relatives are not aware of the fate that befell a long-lost relative.

The Royal British Legion has performed invaluable work in commemorating all men, and in more modern times women, who have fallen in action. The Legion has been supportive of the call for pardons, which were granted to those men who deserted from both the World Wars and remained at liberty, by the newly crowned Queen Elizabeth II in 1953.

Those deserters who were apprehended during the Great War were not punished in this country: they were shipped back to France or Belgium and were dealt with there. They were treated in the same way as those who had deserted and submitted themselves to the authorities, as in the case of Neath's William Jones. Whilst attending the dedication service when his name was placed on Glynneath's War Memorial, sitting talking to the author, George Brinley Evans and to Tom Marston, George in his laconic way said:

> Imagine the scene all those years ago: William Jones' mother saying to him, 'Now, Will, bach, this is not right. Go back, tell them you made a mistake, they will understand.' He did, of course, but not much understanding was evident, once he was shipped back to the Front, he was not going to see the Vale of Neath in Glamorgan again. He was shot.

The least we can do is to remember all those men who fell on The Western Front. No matter how they died. The old men who hobbled about the street for years following the

Great War, often ridiculed by children, bore the hardships that one would have to experience to understand; fire scarred faces, a limb or more missing, breathing difficulties because of the gas, and sadness that emanated from their eyes like potash in a burned out hole.

The Great War –great in name only.[53]

Lolita McAllister's poem dedicated to a great uncle:

That field of poppies looks so sweet, so beautiful to see,
It wasn't like that years ago for John and Dave and me.
We knew that we could never have the lives you do today,
And we just had to do our bit, for very little pay.
We knew and felt that we must fight for futures to be free
It wasn't like this then you know for John and Dave and me,
    we gave our all
Nay, more than that, for peace we'd never see,
To make a better world they said to John and Dave and me.
My God, you should have seen it there, where slime and filth
    ran free,
And dead and dying everywhere, with John and Dave and me.
'Gas, gas, boys,' shouted little Tom, and drowned in the melee,
While souls and spirits cried and howled, like John and Dave
    and me.
And then it came in green, foul gusts. In clouds of two or three,
And seeped into the bunker of John and Dave and me.
Our masks had gone some time before, lost in the bloody battle,
So eyes a'water, skin red hot, our voices dried to rattle,
And gasping, searing pain, as lungs in agony did struggle,
To breathe clean air, just one last heave, as insides start to bubble.
But then a sound came from afar, and what a sight to see,
As Angels came to stand on par, with John and Dave and me.
Our spirits rarely come here now, to Flanders Fields so free,
I wonder will you think of us, of John and Dave and me.[54]

A Welsh Dragon proudly looks across the site of Mametz Wood; in those early weeks of the Battle of the Somme the 38th Welsh Battalion lost 4,000 men and so the spot is forever Welsh.

On 12 June 1928, the Welsh Book of Remembrance was inscribed by Prince Edward of Wales in Cardiff. In its pages are recorded the 35,000 Welsh men and women who paid the ultimate price in the Great War. One hopes that those fifteen men who died alone, tied to a stake, are numbered with them.

Endnotes

[1] *In Flanders Fields*, Leon Wolff, p.153

[2] *For the Sake of Example*, Anthony Babington, p.121

[3] *Blindfold and Alone*, Cathryn Corns & John Hughes-Wilson

[4] *In Flanders Fields*, Leon Wolff, p.157

[5] *Blindfold and Alone*, Cathryn Corns & John Hughes-Wilson, p.75

[6] *For God's Sake Shoot Straight*, Leon Sellers

[7] *In Flanders Fields*, Leon Wolff, p.153

[8] *In Flanders Fields*, Leon Wolff, p.154

[9] Author's collection

[10] Author's collection

[11] Author's collection

[12] *Blindfold and Alone*, Cathryn Corns & John Hughes-Wilson, p.259

[13] *Blindfold and Alone*, Cathryn Corns & John Hughes-Wilson, p. 259

[14] Section 12 of the Army Act

[15] Glynneath Branch of the Royal British Legion, private papers, Brian Baker

[16] Royal British Legion

[17] *John Bull* magazine, February 1918

[18] W.E. Bland, Leeds University, Liddle Collection ref. 436 1977

[19] University of Leeds, Liddle Collection, taped recollections ref. 387 1976

[20] *For God's Sake Shoot Straight*, Leon Sellers, p.52

[21] *John Bull* magazine, February 1918

[22] PRO Kew Nelson Battalion War Diary Ref. ADM 156/24

[23] *Officer's Service 1914–1919, Volumes One & Two*, MOD Royal Naval Division Books, Whitehall Library 182/183

24 MOD Whitehall Library 182/183

25 MOD Whitehall Library 192/183

26 MOD Whitehall Library 182/183

27 MOD Whitehall Library 182/183

28 PRO Kew: ADM 156/24

29 PRO Kew: ADM 156/24

30 MOD Whitehall Library 182/183

31 *The Manual of Military Law*, p.18

32 PRO Kew Ref. ADM 156/24

33 PRO Kew Ref. ADM 156/24

34 PRO Kew. Ref. 156/24

35 PRO Kew Ref. 156/24

36 PRO Kew Ref. 156/25

37 *Shot at Dawn*, Julian Putkowski & Julian Sykes, p.155

38 *John Bull* magazine, February 1918

39 *John Bull* magazine, February 1918

40 Leeds University, Liddle Collection taped recollections, J. Blacklock, 1971

41 *John Bull* magazine, February 1918

42 *For God's Sake Shoot Straight*, Leon Sellers, p.80-1

43 PRO Kew Ref. ADM 137/3065

44 Imperial War Museum, Department of Documents – Thomas Macmillan collection

45 *The Hangman's Record*, Steve Fielding, Volume Three 1930–1964, p.119

46 *Shot at Dawn*, Julian Putkowski & Julian Sykes, p.33

47 PRO WO 71/437

48 Hansard, 2006, Contains Parliamentary information licensed under the Open Parliament Licence v1.0

49 Hansard, 2006, Contains Parliamentary information licensed under the Open Parliament Licence v1.0

50 *For the Sake of Example*, Anthony Babington, p.202

51 *For the Sake of Example*, Anthony Babington, p.202

52 *For the Sake of Example*, Anthony Babington, p.203

53 Author's collection

54 With thanks to Lolita McAllister

Executed Soldiers
in Regimental Order

19459	Cpl George Povey	11.2.1915	1/Cheshire Regiment
	Sub Lt Edwin Dyett	5.1.1917	Nelson Battalion Royal Naval Division
12942	L-Cpl William Price	15.2.1915	2/Welsh Regiment
11967	Pte Richard Morgan	15.2.1915	2/Welsh Regiment
10874	Pte James Carr	7.2.1916	2/Welsh Regiment
12727	Pte John Thomas	20.5.1916	2/Welsh Regiment
36224	Pte James Skone	15.5.1918	2/Welsh Regiment
8139	Pte George Watkins	15.5.1917	13/Welsh Regiment
10958	Pte Major Penn	22.4.1915	1/Royal Welsh Fusiliers

10853	Pte Anthony Troughton	22.4.1915	1/Royal Welsh Fusiliers
15954	Pte William Jones	25.10.1917	9/Royal Welsh Fusiliers
15437	Pte Charles Knight	15.11.1915	10/Royal Welsh Fusiliers
1/15134	Pte Anthony O'Neil	30.4.1916	1/South Wales Borderers
44174	Pte William Scholes	10.8.1918	2/South Wales Borderers
11490	Pte T. Henry B. Rigby	22.11.1917	10/South Wales Borderers

Burial Places or Commemorations of the Executed Welshmen

10459	Cpl George Povey	11.2.1915	Menin Gate Memorial*
12942	L-Cpl William Price	15.2.1915	Bethune Town Cemetery
11967	Pte Richard Morgan	15.2.1915	Bethune Town Cemetery
10958	Pte Major Penn	22.4.1915	Estaires Communal Cemetery
10853	Pte Anthony Troughton	22.4.1915	Estaires Communal Cemetery
15437	Pte Charles W. Knight	15.11.1915	La Grand Hazard Military Cemetery
10874	Pte James Carr	7.2.1916	Auchel Communal Cemetery

1/15134	Pte Anthony O'Neil	30.4.1916	Mazingarbe C. Cem. Extension
12727	Pte John Thomas	20.5.1916	Mazingarbe C. Cem. Extension
*	Sub Lt Edwin Dyett	5.1.1917	Le Crotoy Communal Cemetery
8139	Pte George Watkins	15.5.1917	Ferme-Olivier Cemetery
15954	Pte William Jones	25.10.1917	Loche Hospice Cemetery
11490	Pte Henry Rigby	22.11.1917	Cite Bonjean Military Cemetery
36224	Pte James Skone	10.5.1918	Hersin C. Cem. Extension
44174	Pte William Scholes	10.8.1918	Borre Cemetery

* No known grave.

Bibliography

Books

Arthur, Max, *Forgotten Voices of the Great War* (London; Edbury Press, 2002)

Babington, Anthony, *For the Sake of Example* (Barnsley; Leo Cooper, 1983)

Blackburne, Harry W., *This Also Happened on the Western Front* (London; Hodder & Stoughton, 1932)

Corns, Cathryn and John Hughes-Wilson, *Blindfold and Alone* (London; Cassell & Co., 2001)

Fielding, Steve, *The Hangman's Record* (Kent; Chancery House Press, 2005)

Graves, Robert, *Goodbye To All That* (London; Jonathan Cape, 1929)

Lee, Brian and Amanda Harvey, *A Postcard from Cardiff* (Stroud; The History Press, 2011)

Moran, John, *The Anatomy of Courage* (London; Constable, 1945)

Putkowski, Julian and Julian Sykes, *Shot at Dawn* (Barnsley; Leo Cooper, 1992)

Sassoon, Siegfried, *Memoirs of an Infantry Officer* (London; Faber & Faber, 1930)

Sellers, Leonard, *For God's Sake Shoot Straight* (Barnsley; Leo Cooper, 1995)

Thurtle, Ernest, *Military Discipline and Democracy* (London; 1920)

Thurtle, Ernest, *Shootings at Dawn: The Army Death Penalty at Work* (London; Victoria House Printing, 1924)

Wolff, Leon, *In Flanders Fields* (London; Longman, Green & Co., 1958)

Newspapers/Magazines

John Bull magazine
The Times newspaper

Website

cwgc.org

Other

Hansard Debates, November 2006

Public Record Office References

10459 Cpl George Povey WO/71/400
12942 L-Cpl William Price No record
11967 Pte Richard Morgan No record
10958 Pte Major Penn WO/71/414
10853 Pte Anthony Troughton WO/71/413
15437 Pte Charles Knight WO/71/437
10874 Pte James Carr WO/71/443
1/15134 Pte Anthony O'Neil WO/71/462
12727 Pte John Thomas WO/71/468
Sub L. Edwin Dyett ADM 156/24
8139 Pte George Watkins WO/71/559
15954 Pte William Jones WO/71/608
11490 Pte Henry Rigby WO/71/618
36224 Pte James Skone WO/71/641
44174 Pte William Scholes WO/71/656

Index

Index

Also from The History Press

GREAT WAR BRITAIN

Great War Britain is a unique new local series to mark the centenary of the Great War. In partnership with archives and museums across Great Britain, the series provides an evocative portrayal of life during this 'war to end all wars'. In a scrapbook style, and beautifully illustrated, it includes features such as personal memoirs, letters home, diary extracts, newspaper reports, photographs, postcards and other local First World War ephemera.